SCOTTISH URBAN MYTHS AND ANCIENT LEGENDS

GRACE BANKS &
SHEENA BLACKHALL

Ruth, Esther, Peter and Josh, thanks for listening!
Love Mum

Dedicated with thanks to Alan Spence for the support given.

First published 2014

The History Press
The Mill, Brimscombe Port
Stroud, Gloucestershire, GL5 2QG
www.thehistorypress.co.uk

British Library Cataloguing in Publication Data.
A catalogue record for this book is available from the British Library.

ISBN 978 0 7509 5622 2

Typesetting and origination by The History Press
Printed in Great Britain

Stories paint colour, texture and depth
onto a flat, blank landscape.
Expression, emotion and the senses give
characters life, breath and movement.

CONTENTS

Foreword 6

To Begin ... 7

The Highlands 10

Aberdeen City 19

Aberdeenshire 27

Perth and Kinross 35

Angus 43

Fife 52

Stirlingshire 61

Edinburgh 69

Lothian 79

The Borders 80

Glasgow City 92

Argyll and the Inner Isles 103

Outer Hebrides 114

Sutherland 119

Orkney 129

Shetland 134

Inverness 138

Wester and Easter Ross 150

A Mix o' Urban Tale Shorties 171

Bibliography 185

FOREWORD

Everybody loves an urban legend, an urban myth. We've all heard them, usually told by someone who insists the story is true, 100 per cent – it happened to the cousin of a friend of somebody they know. These myths are an important part of our oral tradition, along with (and often including) the ghost story, the yarn, the tall tale.

These stories are universal, the same themes and motifs occurring in many different cultures, and they tend towards the archetypal, the apocryphal. They reflect something profound, those deep structures by which we frame and understand experience. But what gives them their power, their magic, their charm and recurring appeal, is the particular detail, the locale, setting the story in time and place.

Scotland has a rich history of such tales, and two of our finest storytellers, Sheena Blackhall and Grace Banks, have joined forces to set down their own versions of their personal favourites. There will be tales here you recognise, stories you've been told (with that assurance that they're absolutely true!) and others that are new to you. There are stories from all over Scotland – rural myths as well as urban – from centuries past and from the present day. There are stories to make you laugh and stories to chill your spine, told (or retold) with a freshness that's invigorating.

The art of storytelling is alive and well.

Alan Spence, 2014

TO BEGIN ...

To Help You Understand ...

When asked to write Urban Legends as part of the UK series, we were told one book would cover the whole of Scotland. We were asked to include the legend of the Loch Ness Monster. Not exactly an urban myth you might say! So this book has become a mix of both urban myths and local legends. And only a few of many are covered here.

This book will take you on a journey around Scotland, to a variety of places where you will meet characters and creatures, some kindly, many not. We just wish there had been room for more!

Grace Banks, 2014

Urban Myths ...

Anecdotes, rumour, gossip ... urban myths can straddle all those categories. Often they are short like fables and can be told quickly in a paragraph or two. Originally, I became hooked on urban myths after reading Paul Smith's *Book of Nasty Legends*. He stated that 'in the real world, not just a single, oral medium transmission is utilised to communicate folklore but any available and relevant media is employed'.

Recently scholars have examined how legends are formed and spread through popular print media and other non-oral methods. I like to think of urban myths as little acorns desperate to grow into oaks where I provide them with knots, gnarls and leaves (see the Chimera Institute 2011). Most writers in this genre draw on global examples, but this book is different; the tales and urban myths are specific to Scotland. It is the land of the mysterious Big Grey Man of Ben Macdhui and murderous clowns loiter in transit vans to inflict the infamous 'Glasgow smile' upon their victims.

Sheena Blackhall, 2014

Local Legends ...

Alan and Cathy Low run a B&B in Ballater. Each night, guests are privileged to enjoy a bedtime story from Cathy. After staying three nights, one woman asked Cathy if she could take her voice away with her. Listening to the rhythm of story, this lady had relaxed and rested mentally and physically for the first time since childhood.

What a simple life-giving remedy – to share a tale, yet such a rare commodity in our screen-fixated world.

Simple fireside evenings
Eyes meet, gleam with treasures shared ...
Tales warmly spoken, familiar, alive
Cherished, polished with use
Known. Loved. Timeless.
Rhythm of life
Stories, vibrant, significant
gave shape, colour and depth
To their surroundings

But unspoken, they
Fade, wither and vanish.
Now silenced.
Words hidden

on dusty, tired pages.
Leaving the land, the people
More bereft. Barren.
But not many see.

Yet in this winter,
Green shoots appear
Caressed into life
Valuing of wisdom
Lessons from nature
Beauty, joy, sorrows
Words, giving shape, colour and depth
To their surroundings.
Timeless.
Rhythm of life.

Grace Banks

With Thanks ...

We are grateful to all of you who have told us your stories; much of this book has come together due to your open-handed generosity. Thank you!

A Wish for You ...

Certain myths and legends grip the human mind with almost obsessive belief or scepticism. In this collection we hope that amidst the strident well-aired tales, some of those that have become whispers may regain their voice and become familiar and loved once more. May they whet your appetite to listen for or seek out the tales around you, the little and the larger, and encourage you to tell them to others.

Grace Banks, 2014

THE HIGHLANDS

✧ Heroes of Old ✧

While exploring books of myths, legends and folk tales I have frequently come across stories of the Fenian or Fian heroes. I was confused how Finn or Fionn's name came up repeatedly as being a Scottish hero of old, yet I had always associated him with Ireland as the giant hero, Fionn Mac Cumhail. And the name Ossian or Oisín came into the mix, known as the son of Fionn. I have discovered there are overlaps between these two and there appear to be landmarks, some of which have association to both. This whole book could be dedicated to these ancient warriors whose origins are certainly Irish. As priests brought religion west, so legends and stories spread. In Scotland the Fionn and Oisín stories abound in the Gaelic-speaking areas of the country, popularised by MacPherson who claimed to have collated ancient manuscripts and written down the oral form of the poet Oisín's words.

To me the backgrounds of Eirinn (Ireland) and Alba (Scotland) seem almost synonymous in the tales, as if there were no sea in between; the uniting element being their chief enemy, the Lochlannaich, the Vikings whom they fought against for their High King.

In this short account, I give a little flavour of the Fenians, in the hope that readers might be encouraged to burrow deeper into the fascinating and rich lore of these heroes, handed down through generations in one way or another. These tales span legend and myth with a few grains of possible fact from the distant past. GB

✧ The Beginning ✧

Many tales are told of Fionn and his great deeds. This simple story is an account of where it all began.

Cumhal was the chief of the Fenians. In a battle between the Fenians and the powerful clan Morna, Cumhal was killed, and Goll, the one-eyed leader of the Morna, became chief of both clans.

Cumhal's wife had just given birth to a son, and knowing Goll would be merciless towards his vanquished foe's newborn, she hid the child away, to be raised in secret.

His guardians named the fair-haired boy Fionn, and as he grew, he flourished and became straight, tall and fearless. As Fionn grew in stature, his deeds were spoken of with awe; he was as fleet as a deer, and deadly accurate with the sling.

Word came to Goll of this young man's exploits, and the chief realised this must be Cumhal's son. He ordered that Fionn be hunted down and killed. His guardians, hearing of the danger, dyed Fionn's hair black. They gave him the name Deimne, and bid him flee for his own safety.

And so Deimne travelled far and wide, and wherever he took service, he would learn the ways of battle. As his strength grew, he was able to wrestle any man to the ground.

But in Deimne's heart, he longed to learn the lessons of wisdom and to search for the beauty of song and music. One day, he came by a river and found a simple hut where a hermit called Finegas lived. Young Deimne asked the old hermit if he might stay awhile and serve him. Finegas agreed but told him nothing of his own reasons for being there.

The hermit had dwelt by the river for many years and fished in the river daily, in the hope of catching the salmon of great wisdom that was said to live within the pool. For years this fish had eaten nuts that had fallen in the water from the overhanging hazel trees. It was believed these nuts had given the salmon great knowledge and discerning ability, and when a man named Fionn caught and ate of this fish, it was said that the wisdom would be passed on to him.

The third day after Deimne's arrival, Finegas felt a tug on his line. As he hauled in the salmon, he knew that this must be the legendary fish at last. Delighted, he asked Deimne to prepare and cook the fish, but not to taste of it before the hermit. The young man obediently did as he was asked, and set about preparations. When the salmon was cooked, it smelled delicious. However, Deimne, seeing a blister on the skin of the fish, pressed it with his thumb. The blister burst and burnt him, and without thinking, he whisked his thumb up to cool it against his front tooth. Immediately, Deimne felt a strange sensation course through his whole being. He felt clearer and more aware of all that was around him. Giving his head a shake, he presented the cooked salmon to his master. Finegas looked at him with piercing eyes. 'You did not eat of the fish, did you?'

'No sir,' Deimne said hurriedly, 'but I burnt my thumb and gave it a sook.'

Finegas sighed, then smiled and shook his head. 'Your name is not Deimne, is it?'

The young man looked at the hermit. 'No sir, it is Fionn.' He quickly explained the reason for changing his name.

The hermit nodded and suddenly burst out laughing. 'You have no idea what you have done, do you?' Fionn shook his head, puzzled. Finegas explained about the salmon of wisdom, and light dawned on Fionn's face. Now he knew why he felt so clear-minded.

From that day on, whenever Fionn wished to know anything, all he had to do was press his thumb to his tooth. In time, Fionn returned to the Fenians and became their chief, but that, as they say, is another story.

✧ The Life of Oisín ✧

In this legend, you will hear just a little of the life of Oisín, and in your imagination you can see from where this eloquent poet drew his inspiration.

Fionn and his men were returning from a day's hunting when they startled a white doe. Fleet of foot it ran away, with men and hounds in hot pursuit. Fionn and his two dogs soon left the others far behind, but even he was growing breathless when the bonny deer disappeared over a small hill with the dogs, Bran and Sceolan, giving chase. When Fionn reached the top, he halted in astonishment. Below him the doe was lying on the grass, with both dogs gambolling around her, licking her nose and ears as if they were pups.

Fionn smiled and shook his head in wonder; this was a deer that no man would kill.

That very night as Fionn lay sleeping, he felt movement in his bed and there, lying beside him, was a beautiful young woman. She thanked Fionn for saving her and explained that she had been the doe. Three years previously an evil magician had put her, Sadhbh, under an enchantment. Fionn in his mercy had rescued her and now she was free.

The two found love in each other's arms and from that day Fionn did not leave his Sadhbh's side.

But one day word came that an enemy approached and although Sadhbh pleaded for Fionn to stay, he had to lead the Fianna in battle. He returned in triumph seven days later to find his lovely lady had disappeared and not one of his people had been able to save her. He demanded to know where his beloved had gone. With great sorrow they explained that while he was away Sadhbh had watched for his return each day. One morning she had heard the sound of a hunting horn and with great joy Sadhbh had looked out and seen the figure of a warrior approaching with two dogs at his side. Overjoyed to see her beloved once more, Sadhbh had run from the safety of the fort to welcome Fionn home and tell him the joyful news that she was expecting their first child. But when she got closer, Sadhbh gave a cry of fear and anguish. This figure was not Fionn but none other than the enchanter in disguise. Swiftly he smote her three times with his rod of yew and immediately Sadhbh became a deer once more. The two dogs changed and turned into fierce, bloodthirsty hounds who gave chase to the fleeing doe. People streamed out of the fort to rescue Sadhbh, but it was too late. The enchanter, the dogs and the deer all vanished into a mist.

Fionn was broken-hearted, and though he continued to lead his Fianna, he searched for his beloved whenever he could. After seven years he gave up hope and gradually returned to hunting with his men. But one warm summer's day while out hunting, the men heard their hounds baying in the forest ahead as if they had cornered a great beast. But when the men approached they saw no sign of danger; there was just a wild, young boy standing naked and bewildered under a great tree. The dogs were called off but Fionn's hounds remained. They gently lay down by the child and fondly licked the boy's arms and face as if he was familiar to them.

The child returned with the hunters but he had no words. Soon he began to learn to speak and before long he was able to recount his tale. From his earliest memory his only companion had been a white doe, who had loved him and shown him how to find food. They had lived simply in a cave where he had been content. Now and again a dark, cruel man would come to their cave and the boy and the deer were very frightened of his power. One day this evil man came and spoke threateningly to the doe. He smote her harshly on the back with his rod of yew and forced the doe to follow him. She had turned and looked at the boy with eyes that held great sorrow; she did not want to leave him. The boy had tried to follow but found he was immobilised. The next thing he knew, he was waking up to the sound of dogs baying around him.

Fionn had no doubt that this boy was his own son and he loved him dearly. He named him Oisín, meaning little fawn, and whenever he looked upon his son's features, he was reminded of his beautiful wife Sadhbh. Oisín grew to become a brave warrior like his father but his greatest gift was in crafting words. Poetry, stories and songs seemed to flow from him, painting pictures of beauty, war, women and great deeds.

The Fianna fought many battles, Oisín as well as any. But one evening as the men were camped around the fire, weary from combat, they heard the sound of hooves approaching. A tall white horse appeared through the wood and upon it sat an upright figure; her hair gleamed gold in the firelight. She was dressed in white and even in the darkness all eyes saw her beauty. Silently every man respectfully rose and Fionn stepped forward and bowed low. The royal maiden came forward and halted her horse before Fionn.

'I have found you, Fionn Mac Coul,' she said in a clear, lovely voice. 'My name is Niamh and I come from the land of Tír na nÓg. From afar I have heard tell of your son Oisín, the gentle brave man who speaks words of silver and sings with a voice of gold.'

She then turned and her eyes searched for the tall young warrior in the firelight. When her gaze alighted on Oisín, she beckoned to him and he walked forward; he could not take his eyes from her beautiful features. In her quiet, seductive voice Niamh told Oisín of her homeland, where no sorrow was known nor did any man grow weary and old, but rather more vigorous and youthful. She asked Oisín to return with her to the land of the forever young and be her husband.

Oisín could not and did not want to refuse. As Niamh had spoken, his heart and his mind were filled with a love for the queenly lady. Willingly he climbed onto the back of her horse, placed his arms around her waist and went with her. Over sea, through storm and waves they rode. They came to a place of beauty and tranquillity where care and age fell away from Oisín as if he had just discarded his old clothes.

The warrior was given a royal welcome, and there was great joy for the young couple. The wedding feast lasted ten days and nights and Oisín and Niamh were deeply in love. Overtime she bore him three beautiful children and Oisín was a good husband and father; yet, at times his wife would see a faraway look in his eye. One day she asked him if he was content. Oisín smiled and answered that he was very happy, yet he desired to look on his land once more and smell the earth of home. Sadly Niamh begged him not to leave her but when she saw he was determined, she agreed to let him go. She warned her husband that many years had passed in the land of his birth and nothing would be as he remembered it. Niamh instructed Oisín that if he wished to return to her then he must on no account ever dismount from his horse or he would regret his actions.

And so Oisín bid farewell to his loving family and rode upon the white horse over the seas to the shores of his homeland. To his dismay he found no trace of his father or any of the Fianna, and when he questioned a passer-by, the man looked at him strangely and frowned. He said he recalled his father speaking about the heroes of old from ancient times, but it was only a distant memory. Greatly disturbed Oisín rode on to the fort where the Fianna had lived, but little remained; only weeds and brambles grew over crumbling ruins. Tears of grief fell down Oisín's cheeks as he thought of all he had lost. Now he regretted leaving his dear Niamh and their children.

But as he pulled on the horse's reins to leave, his eye caught sight of a water trough filled with rainwater and suddenly he smiled. This was where he and the Fianna used to wash their hands. On impulse he eagerly dismounted to use the trough one last time, but as his feet touched the grass he collapsed and all strength went from his limbs. Age and decrepitude fell upon Oisín's frame; he was so weak he could do nothing. Too late he remembered Niamh's warning and dismayed, he watched as the white horse turned, galloped from the glade and vanished. He tried to cry out for his comrades but his voice was cracked and reedy. He lay there for a long time, broken, sorrowful and dried out. But Oisín was not finished. He found a hazel branch and with difficulty raised himself up and feebly shuffled out from the forest. Some peasants found the frail, bent white-haired giant and took him to the home of a nearby priest.

The priest was called Patrick; he treated Oisín kindly and listened to his tales of old. The aged man spoke sadly and eloquently of times long past; the hunting and the thrill of the chase, the camaraderie of the Fianna, the wonder of spring buds and birdsong, and the joy and companionship of women. In the years that remained to Oisín, it is said that the priest tried to persuade the man to take the faith, but the poet stubbornly refused. To his last breath, Oisín's whispers were of those he loved, of the Fianna, of Niamh and of his children.

Sites in Scotland named after the Fenian heroes

Here I briefly mention a few of the Scottish sites associated with Oisín, but I respectfully acknowledge that in Eirinn many more are to be found.

Ossian's Cave was where the poet was supposedly born. Even today, climbers consider access to this cave a difficult and dangerous climb. It is referred to as Ossian's Ladder. It is not a cave as such, but more of a recess in the cliff face about the length of a bowling alley.

Clach Ossian is a great boulder, eight feet in height. When General Wade sought to make a straight road through the Sma Glen this massive stone barred the way. With great difficulty it was shifted, and beneath it a grave was found, containing shards of bones and ashes. These were presumed to be Oisín's remains. In honour of the great and well-loved bard, men gathered with great solemnity to lay Oisín's bones to rest high in the hills of Glen Almond.

Loch Ossian is situated at the north-east side of Rannoch Moor and is surrounded by hills and mountains. There are no roads to this place, but the railway takes you to Corrour. From here, access to the loch is by footpath.

Pobull Fhimm, or Fionn's People, are standing stones that lie seven miles south of Lochmaddy Langais near Clachan in North Uist.

Suidhe Coire Fhionn, or the place of Fionn's cauldron, is in Arran and was the site of a cooking pot where Fionn and the Fenians cooked their deer. Two circles of boulders make up this site and a small cist has been found underneath.

Sòrnaichean Coir' Fhìnn, or the fireplaces of Fionn, can be found near Kensaleyre in Skye.

ABERDEEN CITY

Aberdeen is the oil capital of Europe. It is also my native city, and has this rather charming epitaph on a headstone in one of its cemeteries:

Here lie the bones of Elizabeth Charlotte
Born a virgin, died a harlot
She was aye a virgin at seventeen
A remarkable thing in Aberdeen SB

✧ Unexpected Consequences ✧ – a tale fae King's College

King's College was commissioned by Bishop Elphinstone, and was the fourth university in Scotland. As the name indicates, it was built with permission from, and in honour of, King James IV. Elphinstone's vision was to bring learning and knowledge to the north. It began with only a few students, who graduated by the age of nineteen and then made their way into academia or the Church.

As the number of students grew, it became necessary to establish and define better rules and regulations. Today College Bounds is still the name of the nearest street to King's, and as such was the containment area for roving students, who also had a curfew to encourage study and curb extreme carousing. The university did not want its name blackened by drunken students tearing across town. Discipline could be an issue when many of the lecturers were only a few years older than those they were teaching.

The university was founded on a strongly held code of beliefs, and thus the students were obliged to adhere to the religious order of prayers, services and scripture learning. If you enter the chapel today, you can see how some of the students spent their time. Over the years they attended chapel, each student must have remained in the same seat. Dating back to 1617 the students have carefully and laboriously carved their names into the wood behind or above their seats. GB

For as long as they have existed, students have persisted in certain pranks and behaviours. However, when Sacrist Downie was given charge over the students at King's, they had met their match. He was shrewd, and seemed to have foreknowledge of all possible routes out of the grounds, while he relished stamping out misdemeanour in all its forms.

The students felt repressed, for Downie showed no lenience. Over the months, high-flung behaviour was curbed, and the students were eventually forced to comply with anything the sacrist demanded. Murmurings grew to whispered mutiny. Grumblings formed into seeds of revenge. Imaginative minds schemed and planned. As details were finalised and word spread of revenge on Sacrist Downie, it was greeted with great enthusiasm.

One late winter's evening, as Downie prowled round on his usual circuit, powerful hands suddenly gripped him tightly and tied his wrists behind him. A cloth was roughly tied in place, gagging him. Struggling in protest, he was dragged to a dimly lit room, where he was propelled to a stool and forced to sit down. As Downie was held there, he became aware of a large number of figures surrounding him. Indignant, he tried to shout through the cloth, but only strange gargled sounds came out. He felt angry and helpless. He tried to turn about to see his captors' faces, but he was forced to face forwards. The room was ominously silent as Downie continued to struggle to get free; the only sounds were his moans and groans. Eventually the man quietened down.

In front of his stool there was a table; sitting behind it were four shrouded figures, no faces could be seen. Downie decided his best chance was to see what this nonsense was all about, and look for the first opportunity to escape and report these young whippersnappers to his superiors.

One of the figures at the table cleared his throat and spoke in a deep, booming voice. 'Downie, you are here to be tried for your misdemeanours and unfair treatment of those under your care. The following witnesses are all willing to testify to your guilt, and by the end of this trial, we hope that you too will see that you are in fact culpable as charged. Let the witnesses be brought forward.'

A line of young men approached the table. Their faces were all familiar to Downie. His anger began to burn in his belly; how dare these impudent rascals treat him in such an undignified manner! One by one, the students came forward and stood in front of the sacrist and clearly stated how Downie had abused his position. Humiliated and helpless, but in no way cowed, Downie found himself trembling with rage. Such insolence! When the line of accusing students had come to an end, Downie's eyes were defiant and sweat was dripping down his face.

Once more the booming voice spoke out from the darkness. 'Downie, you have heard the charges pronounced against you by these witnesses, you have been convicted of your crimes, now comes your judgement.'

In vain, Downie struggled for the right to be heard, but the cloth around his mouth muffled any sound he tried to make. It was almost as if he was not actually present. He felt powerless, and as the voice continued, for the first time he felt a frisson of cold fear.

The voice said, 'Your punishment is death by beheading.'

Suddenly the sacrist ceased to struggle. He stared at the table and the figures behind it. He must have misheard. Surely? He looked wildly around the room for a sign of laughter. This was ridiculous!

It was all a prank … was it not? Downie felt panic rising; a hysterical high-pitched whine was heard through the gag, while the man pleaded with his eyes for it all to stop.

Hands raised him up and pulled a black hood roughly over his head. Downie felt completely claustrophobic, almost as if he were drowning. It was a struggle to breathe, and his heart was racing uncontrollably. Feebly, he moaned and staggered between his captors. Strong arms hauled him forward a short distance until he was thrust down, this time upon his knees.

Through the black cloth, he was horrified to hear the sound of metal being sharpened. Desperately, he tried to struggle to his feet, but his bound hands hampered him, and he collapsed to his knees and his head slammed against a wooden block that had been placed in front of him. Hands held him down.

'And so Downie, to your execution!' The words were pronounced coldly, but to the prisoner, it felt like he was hearing them from afar.

The student beside the kneeling sacrist took a wet cloth and whipped it lightly across Downie's bare neck. He grinned as the body below him slumped forward and fell to the ground in an ungainly manner.

He looked around at the crowd behind him. Everyone was nodding, smiling with satisfaction, except for one. This student was looking at the still body of the sacrist, lying inert and undignified. Swiftly, he stepped forward and knelt down beside Downie's head. He whipped off the hood and gasped. It felt like time stood still. All seemed suspended. Wildly, he turned, his eyes full of terror. 'I think he's dead!'

The gag was removed, and the students tried desperately to fill the sacrist's lungs with air, but Downie was gone, his heart unable to cope with the trauma he had experienced.

It was agreed by all present that the night's activities would never be retold until the very last of them had reached old age. The body of the sacrist was smuggled out from the university grounds and buried in a lonely area known as Berryden.

In 1824, the story was published of how Aberdeen students had put their porter on trial and then murdered him. This tale seemed to gather momentum and reappeared in print through the nineteenth and into the twentieth century.

'Airt and part in Downie's slaughter' became a well-known saying, meaning confederates will not inform on one another. As to Downie's memory, a stone tribute to the sacrist can be seen, obscurely placed in bushes outside of Seaton Park, north of the university.

✧ Of Little Girls and Dolls ✧

A travelling woman called Esther Stewart worked in a fish house in Aberdeen. In 1947, two years after the war had ended, Mrs Stewart's little daughter Charlotte was very ill. SB

Esther and her husband occasionally hawked round the doors of the city to make ends meet; one particular night they came to a huge house belonging to a colonel. Esther's husband had been a soldier in the army and the colonel had been his senior officer. The couple were asked in and there in the hall Esther caught sight of a most beautiful lifesize doll. The colonel had bought it in America for his daughter, who was now a married woman living away from home. The doll resembled the fairy from The Wizard of Oz; it had pale skin, long golden hair, blue eyes and wonderfully made clothes. Esther was very taken with the doll, and the colonel's wife was delighted to gift it to her daughter.

When Esther arrived home, she gave the doll to Charlotte, who was thrilled to be given such a beautiful gift, but at night-time her mother insisted that because Charlotte was ill and the doll so large, the doll must sit on a chair beside Charlotte's bed. The next morning Esther was annoyed to find Charlotte sleeping with the huge doll in her arms, but Charlotte insisted the doll had come by itself. Every night it was the same. Esther tried putting the doll at the bottom of

Charlotte's cot, but the same thing happened: in the morning it was back in the little girl's arms.

At first, the travellers thought this was their daughter's imagination, but gradually they noticed Charlotte's health was not improving; her cough had become worse and she looked pale and fevered. The parents took their daughter into their own bed. That night they were woken by a cry of 'Mamma!' To their horror they found the doll had managed to move up from their daughter's cot and had crawled in between them to be with Charlotte. For the next week the parents tried everything to stop the doll from climbing into bed beside them, but they could not prevent it.

The couple decided the doll was damaging to Charlotte; it was evil and seemed possessed of a soul. The doll must go! Charlotte was heartbroken to be parted from her doll, but Esther was firm; she would return it to the colonel's house. When Esther explained what had happened, the colonel's wife paled. Hesitantly she explained that when their daughter had left home to be married, she had taken the doll with her. But during the night, the doll had made its way into the newly married couple's bed; when they woke up they found it lying between them. Both she and her husband were so alarmed, they hastily packed up the doll and returned it to the family home. The doll was banished to the attic but inexplicably, every morning, it was found outside their daughter's door, crying 'Mamma!' For some time the colonel and his wife been trying to find another home for it. Esther was relieved to be rid of the doll and although Charlotte was distressed to lose it, her health began to improve and before long she had fully recovered.

✧ The White Dove Inn ✧

A famous child ghost used to haunt the White Dove Inn near St Swithin's Street, Aberdeen. Here is the tale as it was told to the psychic Elliott O'Donnell by a Nurse Mackenzie. SB

On one occasion Nurse Mackenzie was sent with Nurse Emmett to the White Dove Inn to look after one of the guests. Each nurse would work back-to-back as day and night nurses. The proprietor did not know much about his paying guest; her name was Miss Vining and she had been an actress. Shortly after arriving at the inn she had fallen ill and the attending doctor had diagnosed her as suffering from a dreaded oriental ailment. Miss Vining's condition had deteriorated rapidly, thus requiring the services of the two nurses.

The patient was an attractive woman, but too ill to talk. Nurse Mackenzie's first night on duty passed uneventfully and by morning Miss Vining's condition seemed to have improved. The following night the weather changed; a fierce storm raged around the inn. Two hours into her vigil, Nurse Mackenzie took the patient's temperature and afterwards picked up a book and settled down in her chair to read. The nurse happened to glance up from her page and spied a small girl in the room. This was decidedly odd, as Nurse Mackenzie had not heard the door open. She assumed that the noise had been muffled by the howling wind outside.

The nurse rose to order her out, for the patient was far too ill for visitors. But the girl held up her hand to stop her. The child was wearing a wide-brimmed bonnet which hid her face. She gave the impression of being graceful, aristocratic and of Eastern origin. The nurse was spellbound. But in her bed Miss Vining was flinging herself back and forth deliriously. The nurse rubbed her eyes, and when she opened them the child had vanished. Miss Vining's temperature had risen to 104°F. In the morning she was slightly calmer. When Nurse Mackenzie told the doctor he was furious.

'Whatever happens, no one must come into the room tonight, not even her daughter, if that is who she was. Miss Vining is far too ill to be disturbed. Make sure and lock the door!'

When night came, the nurse locked the door as ordered and sat by the fire. There was no wind now, only heavy, steady falling snow, which laid an eerie silence over the sleeping world.

At quarter to one, a sob of terror and pain came from the bed. There by Miss Vining stood the child. Nurse Mackenzie was frozen with fear. However, with a great effort she roused herself. 'Who are you? Tell me your name now! How dare you enter this room uninvited?'

The child lifted her head and the nurse snatched off the wide-brimmed bonnet. It dissolved in her hands into empty air. She realised with horror that she was looking down at the corpse of a Hindu child with a huge seeping cut in its throat. Once, it had been a lovely little girl, now hideously ravaged by death and dissolution. With a shriek of horror the nurse fainted from sheer fright. When she revived, the ghostly apparition had vanished and Miss Vining lay dead, her hands shielding her face in the moment of dying.

Nurse Mackenzie had to gather Miss Vining's possessions together to see if she could discover some clue as to the deceased's next of kin, but all she could find was a photograph of the Hindu girl on a postcard. It had a postmark from Quetta on the back, and the words, 'Natalie ... may God forgive us both'. Despite thorough and prolonged inquiries, no trace of the girl or the dead woman's origins was ever discovered.

ABERDEENSHIRE

✧ The Tusk ✧

When I was barely the height of nothing, I shared a bed with my grandmother Lizzie, who was very old and a great storyteller. Sometimes, if I pestered her for long enough, she would tell me about some of the members of her 'rogue's gallery' from Scotland's past, and here is one of them. SB

In the ninth century, in the Highlands of Mar, there lived an earl (mormaer) by the name of Maelbrigda; he was nicknamed 'The Tusk' because of a huge, protruding sharp front tooth.

One day Maelbrigda encountered the notorious Viking, Sigurd of Moere, first Earl of Orkney. In AD 839 the two warriors agreed to fight, with forty men and forty horses each. Sigurd was a wily Norseman and cheated by placing two warriors on each of the forty horses.

All the men of Mar were killed and beheaded; the heads were taken as prizes by the Vikings and attached to their saddles. Sigurd sliced off Maelbrigda's head, but as he was riding off in triumph, the famed 'tusk' tooth sank into Sigurd's thigh. In life Maelbrigda had never been fastidious in matters of dental hygiene, and his filthy tooth caused Sigurd's wound to fester. As a result the Viking died and is buried in Orkney, the first ever man to be killed by dental caries.

✧ The Big Grey Man of Ben Macdhui ✧ – a legend fae the Cairngorms

I have found that if you want a good story, hill walkers and climbers will deliver. While travelling around and hostelling in pursuit of legends for this book, I met a number of people who had ghostly encounters to tell or had heard one from a fellow climber. Of all these tales, the Big Grey Man, or, in Gaelic, Am Fear Liath Mòr, is the most widely known. Ben Macdhui in the Cairngorm Mountains has been the site of encounters with Am Fear Liath Mòr for many years. But some time ago, I was in an outdoor shop in Aberdeen when I heard two teenagers talking, who were off to climb a small local hill near their town.

'Aye, we'd best watch out for the Big Grey Man the morn!'

'What?'

'Aye, my ma says she saw it when she was climbing Bennachie!'

As with other strange and obscure phenomena, there may be plenty of sightings of Am Fear Liath Mòr that have gone unrecorded, but his authenticity has apparently been verified and documented by some prominent individuals over the years. GB

In 1891, Professor Norman Collie was climbing in the Cairngorms. He was a chemistry lecturer based at University College in London, and loved to be away from the city to embrace the clear mountain air of his native Scottish Highlands. He was an experienced climber and well respected amongst mountaineers of his day.

One morning, Collie took a fancy to climbing Ben Macdhui. He had made good progress despite poor visibility; the cloud was low and he had to consult his compass continually. He reached the summit and stopped for a brief snack, but the air was cool and he wanted to keep moving. Collie set off back downhill, but after about ten minutes' descent, he felt a shiver going down his spine. As he walked, he could hear a tread that was not his own, and, disturbingly, for every three of his footsteps, it was taking just one stride.

Collie was a great believer in the supernatural, and had always enjoyed a good mystery or a yarn, but suddenly all the horrors and dread of what 'it' could be crowded into his head, and although he tried to shake off his discomfort, he found it extremely hard to keep calm. He tried to think rationally, for he knew that in low cloud sound could be deceptive, but Collie became more and more convinced that whatever it was, it was pursuing him. His steps quickened, and he looked around wildly, but could see nothing for the mist. Collie panicked, all reason fled; he ran all the way back down, as fast as scree and boulders would allow. It was four or five miles to Rothiemurchus Forest but he never stopped until he was down.

It took thirty-four years for Collie to relate his experience in public, which he did to the members of the Cairngorm Club at their annual general meeting in 1925. As Collie's tale was circulated, it encouraged others to tell of their own encounters; it seemed many people had experienced similar incidents.

In the 1920s, two competent climbers, Alexander Mitchell Kellas and his brother, spent the day climbing up Ben Macdhui. As they approached the summit, they saw before them something moving up from the Lairig Ghru pass. The brothers stopped, astounded; this was no ordinary climber but a large, monstrous figure. It climbed with huge, effortless strides to the summit, circled round the cairn, its head level with the top of the ten-foot stone mound, before disappearing back down the way it had come. The Kellas brothers had no doubt in their minds; they had both seen the creature. The Am Fear Liath Mòr was no figment of the imagination.

In October 1943, Alexander Tewnion was out hunting on the mountain. As Tewnion was traversing the Coire Etchachnan, a blanket of fog descended around him. Without warning, a huge figure charged through the swirling mists towards him. Instinctively, the hunter reached for his revolver and fired three shots, but the creature was not deflected, and Tewnion turned and ran, not stopping until he reached Glen Derry.

In his many visits to Ben Macdhui since that day, whether walking or camping, Tewnion never encountered the Am Fear Liath Mòr again, nor felt in the least perturbed on any occasion, for he was convinced that on that dark day in October he had actually killed it.

In the early 1950s, Peter Densham, who had been leader of the Cairngorms RAF rescue team from 1939 to 1945, was out climbing Ben Macdhui. There had been a constant, low, heavy mist, and all through the day the light had been poor. He was beginning his descent when he heard footsteps close by. He stopped to listen; he could feel his heart hammering in his chest. The shrouded mountain was eerily quiet apart from the sound of the wind skiffing the boulder-strewn moonscape that he knew was around him.

Densham was unconsciously holding his breath as he tentatively stepped forward, and suddenly he heard the footsteps begin again. He tried to stifle the clawing fear, speaking rationally to himself, but the sense of dread and foreboding was so overwhelming that his body took flight, veering away from whatever it was that was chasing him. Driven by his fear, Densham was propelled from the path, coming dangerously close to falling off the edge of the cliff. It took great willpower for him to change direction and make his way safely down the mountain. When reflecting on his experience, Densham could not tell in those circumstances whether what he had heard and felt was real, or a distortion of natural phenomena, where his mind was wrestling with the unknown.

Wading through the legends ...

What phenomenon could inspire such stories? And all from the same area! Footsteps where there should be none, an overwhelming sense of oppressive doom, or a malignant presence, and for some, the sighting of a huge figure or creature.

Nature's Voice

A lack of oxygen is a possible explanation for these experiences. The mountain is relatively high, remote and stark, and it is easy to become disorientated. The weather contributes to this, as cloud often shrouds its features. On a remote mountain such as Ben Macdhui, the lack of visibility, the constant near-silence, and the isolation will heighten a person's sensitivity to sound, and contribute to anxiety. Indeed, the imagination can start to change the sounds of wild animals and that of rock and mountain into something unknown and frightening, and even fabricate them entirely.

Inexplicable Footprints

There was one man, John A. Rennie, who came across giant footsteps in the snow, fifteen miles from Ben Macdhui, in the Spey Valley. In his book *Romantic Strathspey*, he describes the footprints as a solitary unbroken line across a stretch of snow on an isolated hillside. They were huge steps, nineteen inches long by fourteen inches wide with about seven feet between each one. Rennie photographed them, and on another occasion, he actually saw the footsteps forming. But as he watched, he realised there was no creature; the 'prints' in the snow were being created by precipitation.

Spectres and Shades

A rare occurrence on Ben Macdhui is a view of a Brocken spectre. From a height, if the clouds part and the light and mist are right, some walkers have seen their own shadow cast onto the mists beyond, which can assume eerily gigantic proportions. Occasionally, this can be accompanied by a halo of rainbow light known as a 'glory'. This very spooky effect could definitely account for some of the Am Fear Liath Mòr sightings, but not all.

Well-known poet and shepherd James Hogg was herding his sheep on the slopes of Ben Macdhui in 1791 when he saw a huge creature close by, thirty feet high. Hogg was so scared that he 'was actually struck powerless with astonishment and terror'. He panicked and ran home, leaving his sheep on the slope. The following day, when he returned to the herd, he saw exactly the same 'blackamoor'. But having pondered on his experience from the previous day, this time he raised his hat off his head. The spectre did exactly the same. Fears allayed, Hogg laughed with relief. For him, the phenomenon was explained; the light and mist were just playing tricks.

Legend or Not?

There is such a mix of accounts about the Am Fear Liath Mòr from clear-headed and respected men. Some people definitely believe there is something roaming on the peaks around Ben Macdhui, while others are convinced Am Fear Liath Mòr is the human mind's method of coping with abnormal or inexplicable freaks of nature. Perhaps a visit to this often-misty mountain is the only way for you to decide whether the Cairngorms do indeed host a creature outwith our ken!

✧ The Horseman's Word ✧

The Society of the Horseman's Word existed in Scotland from the eighteenth century up to the early twentieth century. Every man who was involved with horses, whether carters, blacksmiths or ploughmen, had to learn the mystical rites which, it was said, gave them power over both horses and women. It was said that the rituals of the Freemasons heavily influenced the Society. My grandfather was a Past Master in the Deeside Lodge of the Masons at Aboyne, and was given a Masonic funeral, attended by his brothers in masonry. The Curlers' Court often passed members of the Horsemen's Word Society and the Freemasons Brethren into another secret society; members were invited to join by personal invitation. SB

In the ceremony of the Horseman's Word, the young candidate, who was usually a ploughboy, was asked to go to the nearest barn between 11 p.m. and 1 a.m. The boy was blindfolded outside the door, and was led into the barn and up to a rough altar, presided over by an experienced horseman, usually flanked by another three horsemen. The candidate would bring a loaf, a bottle of whisky, a candle and, if he had money, a pound. Then, he would have to answer a series of questions:

'Who caught the first horse?'

'It was Adam.'

'Where did he catch him?'

'At the east side of the Garden of Eden, on the way to the Land of Nod.'

At the end of the questioning, the initiate had to shake the Devil's hand, often a stick covered with hairy skin, before being given the magic words; the Horseman's Word was 'Baith in Een', meaning Both in One.

Thereafter came the oath of secrecy … and what an oath it was!

> I do now and ever swear before the Almighty God and all these witnesses that I shall always heal, conceal and never reveal any part of the secret of horsemanship which is about to be revealed to me this night. Furthermore I solemnly vow and swear that I will neither write it nor indite it, cut it nor carve it, nor engrave it on wood, sand or snow, parchment, stone, brick, tile clay or anything movable under the whole canopy of heaven nor yet so much as wave one single letter with a finger in the air from which anything may be known there-from. Furthermore I vow and swear that I will never give it nor see it given to a tradesman of any kind except to a veterinary surgeon or a horse soldier. Likewise I shall never give it nor see it given to a farmer or farmer's son unless he be working his own or his father's horses.

Furthermore I will never give it or see it given to a fool or a madman, nor to a drunkard, nor to any man who would abuse his own or his master's horse with it nor to anyone below the age of 18 or above the age of 45; nor to my father, mother, sister or brother, wife nor witch nor to any womankind. Furthermore I will never give it or see it given to anyone after sunset on Saturday night nor before sunrise on Monday morning. Furthermore I will neither abuse nor bad use any man's horses with it and if I see a brother do so I will tell him of his fault.

Furthermore I will never advise anyone to get it nor disadvise anyone from getting it but leave everyone to his own free will and accord. Furthermore I will never see it given nor give it for less than one pound sterling, a loaf and a bottle of whisky and I will never give it nor will give it unless there be three or more sworn lawful brethren present after finding them to be so by trying and examining them. Furthermore I will never refuse to attend a meeting if warned within three days except in exceptional circumstances such as a house on fire, riding for a doctor, or a woman in travail. If I fail to keep these promises may my flesh be torn to pieces by wild horses and my heart cut through with a horseman's knife and my bones buried beneath the sands of the seashore where the tide ebbs and flows every twenty-four hours so that there may be no remembrance of me amongst my lawful brethren. So help me God, Amen.

My uncle told me that the Society of Esoteric Endeavour produced a volume named *The Society of the Horseman's Word* which included some nineteenth- and twentieth-century texts from this society. It was a limited edition of only 1,000 copies and the first 100 contained an envelope with a hank of horsehair knotted in the traditional way; this symbol was given as an invitation for members to join the Brethren.

PERTH AND KINROSS

✧ The Coffin Wrangle ✧ – a legend fae Glenshee

The story of 'The Shearer of Glenshee' has been told for generations by the Stewarts of Blair, who were travellers from Perthshire. Sheila Stewart kindly gave me permission to tell this intriguing tale, which comes from the area she and her family knew so well. GB

Many years ago, a man called John Stewart was seeking work. He had heard berry-pickers were needed in Perthshire, so he travelled there, and for six weeks he worked in the fields around Blairgowrie. By September the berry crop was harvested, and John was prepared to move on, but the other workers persuaded him to stay and share a mug of ale with them. One drink led to another and very quickly they had cleared John out of his savings.

Feeling wretched, John left the next day, making for Glenshee. He was told there was plenty of work on the farms at that time of year. But in the glen, a freak snowstorm roared down from the north, and within moments, he was in a complete whiteout. He could not even see his hands in front of his face. John had to find shelter, and quickly. He bore on into the biting cold blizzard, his fingers and face frozen as the wind howled around him. At one point, the whirling snow gusted aside and in the distance he was relieved to see a light. He laboured towards it through the drifts; his clothes and hat caked white with snow. Little by little, he struggled closer to the light, and finally he was knocking at the door of a small croft.

An old man opened the door and welcomed the frozen man in; he and his wife gave John a seat by the fire, wrapped him in warm blankets and fed him a plate of thick, hot broth. John slept by the fire that night, but come morning the old man asked him if he would be able to stay and work around the croft. The man was getting too old for heavy labouring and could use the help. He could not pay John, but if he was willing, he could provide bed and board; there was a shed John could use at the bottom of the garden. He readily agreed, and the couple were very pleased.

John was a good labourer and worked hard for a few months, but come early spring, he was thinking to move on. However, the lambing and shearing season was beginning, and the old man told him there would be plenty of work in the glen if he wanted to stay. John was easily persuaded; he was happy to remain. The couple were pleased; they had become very fond of John; he was like a son to them.

For the whole of that spring, John went up and down the glen, and over to Glen Isla too, tirelessly helping with the lambing. He was becoming a familiar figure in both glens.

When the time came for the shearing, the old man showed John how the job was done, and very quickly, John became a deft hand, shearing as well as the next man. Soon he was shearing three or four sheep to another man's one; he was just a natural.

John's expertise grew in demand across the glens. He was a hard worker and took care to do his work thoroughly. By the end of the season, the folk of the glens had come to like and respect him, and he became known as the Shearer of Glenshee. So John lived in the glen for some years, content to stay in the wee shed belonging to the old couple.

One afternoon, John had asked to take the old man's dog out on the hill. The day had started fine but the weather deteriorated quickly; thick cloud suddenly blanketed the mountains and the heavens opened. Within moments, both man and dog were soaked to the skin, and in the fog, John had no idea which direction to head safely back down to the glen.

When John had not returned by evening, the couple grew anxious. The old man checked the shed several times, but there was no sign of man or dog.

During the night, John eventually stumbled back down to the croft. He was completely done in, cold to the bone and shivering uncontrollably; he could hardly function. John could think of nothing but crawling into his bed to sleep; he did not even think to take off his sodden clothes. The shivering dog silently lay down at the bottom of the bed.

By morning, the couple were very worried. John had not appeared for breakfast. The old man went down to the shed and was horrified to find the shearer in his bed, delirious, and shaking violently, his skin burning to the touch. John's bed was wringing wet, his clothes clung to his skin. The doctor was called for, but to no avail, it was too late. John had double pneumonia and would not recover.

Devastated, the couple nursed John tenderly, but he never regained consciousness, and he died in the middle of the night.

There was shock and great sadness up and down the glens as word spread of the shearer's death. The day of the burial came, and the coffin was hoisted onto willing shoulders and carried down the glen to be buried in Glenshee kirkyard.

The funeral bearers approached the crossroads where the kirk stands on one side of the road and the road to Glen Isla veers off on the other.

Standing there waiting was a crowd of men with weapons and tools. As the two groups faced one another, the Glen Isla men began to bicker resentfully at the Glenshee funeral procession. They were adamant they had as much right to bury the shearer in their kirkyard as did the Glenshee folk! The coffin was gently placed down until the impasse was resolved.

It took only one threatening word, and tempers flared quickly on both sides. Soon folk from both glens were battering away at each other; it was a dreadful fight. But as the men raged against one another, darkness fell about them and they could see nothing. The men ceased to fight, and an unearthly hush fell upon them. All was still; even the birds were silent.

After some time, the pitch-blackness began to lighten and lift and the sun broke through, showing many of the men badly hurt. Suddenly, one man cried out in fright, 'Oh my God, look what's happened! Look what's happened!' Everyone looked to where the man was pointing. At the roadside where the coffin had been placed, there were now two coffins. All dispute forgotten, the people gathered round, awestruck by the sight. The two coffins were so similar; there was seemingly no difference between them. The nameplates were exactly alike; they both had the shearer's name and age on them. And when they lifted the coffins, there was no difference in weight between the one and the other.

After a time, the Glen Isla folk quietly lifted up one coffin and returned to their glen to bury the shearer, while the folk of Glenshee did likewise in their own kirkyard. But still to this day, no one actually knows in which coffin lie the remains of the Shearer of Glenshee.

✧ From Around the Fortingall Yew ✧ – legends fae Glen Lyon

Some 5,000 years ago in a beautiful glen in the central highlands of Scotland, a tiny berry fell from a yew tree, was buried in the ground and took root. Today, a tree still survives here, the oldest in Britain, and among the oldest in Europe. This is the Fortingall Yew, situated beside a little church in Glen Lyon. At first glance, it looks as if there are a number of trees here, not just one, but this solitary yew has endured despite centuries of harmful folk traditions, and still sends out new twigs every year. Many believed it to be a tree of power. As such, it was known as the tree of knowledge, and burning fires in its centre was common practice. In 1854, Louden described the Fortingall Yew as having its very heartwood burnt from its centre, and funeral processions would move through the archway that remained.

In the eighteenth century, the girth of the Fortingall Yew was measured at 56 feet. Today, white pegs define the trunk's original circumference. For centuries, yew wood was the favoured choice for making bows. How many of this tree's branches were used for this purpose? In the nineteenth century, a 'tourist industry' of sorts was flourishing; locals removed branches for making into quaichs and other trinkets for visitors. Eventually, a stone dyke was placed around the tree to protect it from further damage.

The name Fortingall probably originates from the Gaelic 'Feart nan Gall', which translates as the 'Stronghold of the Strangers'. As you travel through Glen Lyon, there is a great sense of history, and not least because of the ancient tree still standing in its midst. This area is brimming with Pictish remains, too. In the 1980s, aerial photography revealed what appear to be crop marks. GB

✧ Roman Visitors ✧

It was around 300 BC that King Mainus decided to make his home in Glen Lyon. His kingdom was large, influential and affluent. During his reign he oversaw the creation of standing stones, stone circles and cup-marked stones, which can still be seen, strewn throughout the glen. One of his descendants was Metallanus, a gentle, humble man, who ruled his people with great wisdom and was well loved in return. The people knew only peace during his reign. However, the glen was well fortified against invasion; there was a string of forts on every hill, equipped with warning beacons, to both the east and west. The king reigned centrally from Dun Geal, the White Fort, at Fortingall.

Living in Glen Lyon, King Metallanus was comfortable with travellers passing through his realm. An astute man, he saw this as a means for trade and newsgathering. Usually people journeyed through the glen from west to east, but one morning, the sentries reported a large contingent of soldiers approaching from the east. They were well armed, but they seemed to come peaceably. The king sent an escort to welcome them directly to his fort.

The men of the glen were people of the earth and stone who knew the beauty of muted heather dyes and bright lichens. When Metallanus first saw the Roman envoys, he was struck by the brilliant hue of their cloaks and the shine of their weapons and armour. The king was courteous and accommodating to his visitors. After they had shared in his hospitality, the Romans explained their reasons for coming to him. They wished to create an alliance with his people, and the king listened, open and interested. They had brought gifts with them, but Metallanus was more concerned with the long-term prospects of this alliance. He saw the opportunity to create trade links and spread his influence through this relationship. He agreed that the Romans could set up camp in the glen, and there they remained peacefully for some time.

As the days and weeks went by, the natives and the Romans mixed as they gathered water, traded goods and worked together to bring in the harvest. Stories and songs were shared around the fireside, feuds were settled, friendships formed, and new relationships bloomed. One of the king's nieces fell in love with a Roman soldier, and their union was duly blessed. Some months later, a child was born, named Pontius Pilate. In the short time he lived in the glen, his favourite place was a yew tree which was close by the Roman camp. He could easily climb on its low, broad branches and rest his head against the warm, reddish brown bark.

When the Romans left Glen Lyon and returned to Rome, Pontius Pilate and his mother went with them. Metallanus was pleased; he wished to widen his understanding of the world. The king ordered a few of his trusted men to go and live in Rome, among them a nephew called Menseteus. They were all instructed to learn as much as they could from the Romans, and return with the knowledge they gleaned. This is exactly what Menseteus did. When he returned to Glen Lyon many years later, he was greeted with great joy. King Metallanus had died by this time, but the new king was enthralled to hear of his relative's experiences and adventures. Menseteus was able to regale his people with stories of the rise of Pontius Pilate and his infamous actions regarding Jesus Christ of Nazareth. Menseteus had become a follower of the Apostle Peter, and he received permission from his king to build a monastery in the glen at Tulli, which over the years became a very important Christian centre for learning.[1]

✧ Miracles from Monks ✧

From the seventh century, Christian monks favoured passage through Glen Lyon as they travelled from Iona in the west to Northumbria in the south-east. One such monk, called Adamnan, was journeying east with a fellow brother, Fillan. When they reached Tyndrum, they drew lots to decide which direction they would journey to preach God's word to the pagan Picts, and build a place for Christian worship.

Adamnan journeyed into the 'Crooked Glen of Stones', as Glen Lyon was known. He settled beside the river at the present Bridge of Balgie and built a mill there. Adamnan was a man of the people; he worked, walked, talked and preached up and down the glen. The people came to love and respect the monk, and they firmly believed in his holy powers.

Some years later, a dreadful plague ravaged the country, killing all in its wake. The people of the glen were terrified to hear it had come as far as the Vale of Fortingall and was infiltrating the glen. In dismay, they flocked to Adamnan, pleading for a miracle to stop the deadly scourge.

Gathering his flock to the hillock where he was accustomed to preach, Adamnan prayed as the plague advanced ever closer. When he lifted his head from prayer, he raised his right arm.

---

1 Here also stood three large stone crosses, to which any criminal could cling for sanctuary.

'I command you, deadly pestilence, to come to me!'

Terrified, the people watched as a cloud began to swarm towards them. 'Now enter this rock,' he ordered, pointing at a rock on the grass below the knoll. Immediately a hole appeared in the rock, and as the onlookers watched, it grew larger as the plague burrowed into its heart.

Ever the practical man, Adamnan ordered his flock up to the shielings on the hillside until he deemed the land to be free from plague. He himself remained in the glen nursing those who were sick and suffering. On returning to their homes, the people of the glen erected a large stone with two crosses on it in memory of the near-disaster from which they had been rescued. They named it Craig-diannaidh, the rock of safety. The rock in which the terrible plague was contained can still be seen close by this standing stone.[2]

At the age of eighty, the beloved monk died, and at his request was carried down the glen on a stretcher. Adamnan had asked that wherever a handle of the stretcher broke, he would be buried at that spot, and a place of worship and learning would be built. The first tie, or 'dull' as it was known, broke at Tulli, where the monastery already stood. Here Adamnan was buried, and the name of the place was changed to Dull, and the church was dedicated to him.[3]

In the centre of Glen Lyon, we return to the wonderful Fortingall Yew. What history this tree has seen, and what stories it could tell from so long ago![4]

---

2 Incised cross slabs such as these are only found in south Argyll, an ancient kingdom of Scotland.

3 In one of the churches in the glen can still be seen a hand bell, similar to ones used in the church on Iona, as well as a font, both from the seventh century.

4 In order to preserve the yew's wonderful heritage, samples have been taken as part of a national project to preserve our ancient trees. These baby 'Fortingalls' (Taxus baccata) were taken to the Botanical Gardens in Edinburgh to form part of a mile-long Yew Conservation Hedge.

ANGUS

✧ The Wicked and the Tragic ✧ – legends fae Glamis Castle

Glamis Castle is the home of the Earl and Countess of Strathmore and Kinghorne, and has housed the Lyon family ever since the fourteenth century. The wife of King George VI, the late Queen Mother, Elizabeth Bowes-Lyon, grew up there, and gave birth to the current Queen's sister, Princess Margaret, in the castle. The castle is near Forfar in the county of Angus in the rich glen of Strathmore. Near Glamis stands the Eassie Stone, carved by the Pictish people. In 1034, King Malcolm II was murdered at Glamis. SB

Earl Beardie

An old Lyon myth from the fifteenth century concerns Alexander, Earl Crawford, who was better known as 'Earl Beardie'. He was a cruel and evil man but was a frequent visitor to Glamis; he often played cards with the second Lord of Glamis, Alexander Lyon. One Saturday night, the two men were gambling and were unaware of the time. It was frowned upon to play cards on the Sabbath and the servants were anxious to tell their master that it was nearing midnight. Eventually the butler plucked up courage and politely interrupted the two men and told them of his concerns. Immediately Lyon acquiesced but the haughty earl was enraged. 'I will play till Doomsday with the Devil himself if he wanted!'

It is said that as everyone left the card room a stranger suddenly appeared and took the seat opposite Earl Beardie, closing the door behind him. One curious servant could not resist looking through the keyhole to see it was Satan himself and immediately the servant was blinded in the eye! At the same time there was a huge clap of thunder, accompanied by a strong whiff of sulphur, and Earl Beardie was seen no more; he had lost his soul to the Devil himself.

The Grey Lady

John Lyon, the sixth Lord of Glamis, was married to Janet Douglas, daughter of the Master of Angus. When he died suddenly, Janet was accused of poisoning her husband; she was denounced as a witch and burned alive in Edinburgh on 17 July 1537. The castle chapel keeps a seat reserved for her ghost, known as the Grey Lady.

Holed Up

Within the castle's 16-foot thick walls was another scene of horrifying deeds, the room of the skulls. The Ogilvie family were tricked into entering the home of their enemy; they were led to a room, grateful for the unexpected hospitality. There they were bricked up to die of starvation.

The Monster of Glamis

The most mysterious of the Glamis Castle myths refers to the Monster of Glamis. Reputedly there was a hideously deformed child of the family who was kept locked up in the castle, and on his death the room where he had lived was bricked up. On one occasion, guests who were staying at Glamis hung towels from every window in the house. When they went outside, there was one window that had no towel visible.

In 1885, a lady called Miss M. Gilchrist described the monster as 'half frog, half man'. She also insisted that he was the rightful earl.

The writer James Wentworth Day, who penned *The Queen Mother's Story* in 1967, alleged that this monster was Thomas Lyon-Bowes, first child of Thomas Lyon-Bowes and Charlotte Grimstead.

In Robert Douglas's *Peerage of Scotland* the child was recorded as 'born and died on October 21st, 1821'. A rumour circulated that the child survived, according to an unnamed midwife. Michael Thornton, another biographer of the Queen Mother, claimed the sixteenth earl told him that Thomas Lyon-Bowes's room had indeed been bricked up after his death. There is no record of where he is buried.

✧ There and Back Again ✧ – the journey of the Stone of Destiny to Arbroath

From even before the time of its status as Scotland's coronation stone, this fabled slab of rock, the Stone of Destiny, is rumoured to have journeyed far. Some say it travelled all the way from the Middle East and was the very rock that Jacob laid his head on at Bethel. More realistically, the stone may have originally been carried over from Tara in Ireland and placed in state at Dunstaffnage in Argyll, the ancient seat of the kings of Scotland. Whatever the case, the stone was later moved to Scone Abbey, and thereafter became the sacred anointing place of Scottish monarchs.

In the reign of King Edward I of England, war and strife ensued, and to Scotland's bitter disappointment, 'Longshanks' brought Scotland to his heel. Not satisfied with this victory alone, Edward was determined to humiliate the Scots further. In 1296, his troops ransacked Scone Abbey, and on the king's orders, seized the stone and had it placed in Westminster Abbey beneath Edward's own specially designed coronation chair. Following the Treaty of Northampton in 1328, England had promised to return the artefact to its Scottish home, but the people of London were outraged at this proposal, and the venture was quickly abandoned. Even when James VI of Scotland united the crowns and became James I of England, a duality that has continued ever since, there was no move to return the stone home to Scone.

Over the years many Scots remained indignant. An artefact and symbol of Scottish sovereignty that most firmly belonged in Scotland (none finer), was still o'er the border. But for all the upset, it still took 655 years for four intrepid students to break into Westminster Abbey and take it back again! GB

In the winter of 1950, Ian Hamilton executed a plan that had been brewing in his mind for a long time. With backing from a few influential men in Glasgow, he and three fellow students travelled south in two cars to take back the Stone of Destiny from Westminster Abbey. Nowadays, this is a straightforward journey, but then the roads were often narrow and dangerous, there was no heating in their cars and the country was in the grip of an icy winter. It was cold, hazardous and they had to use alcohol to stop the windscreen from freezing over.

The plan was for Ian to conceal himself near St Edward's Chapel within the abbey. This was where the stone was kept, enclosed beneath King Edward's Chair. Once the abbey was closed for the night, he would emerge and let the others in. As it happened, he was discovered by the watchman and had to bluff his way out, saying he had been locked in. As he conversed with the man, Ian had to prevent the crowbar he was carrying from slipping down his coat and clattering onto the stone floor. The guard questioned him, but ultimately wasn't suspicious of Ian, and even asked if he was okay for money.

Their opportunity was lost but the team resolved to try again the following night. They had little in the way of funds, so even though it was bitterly cold, they chose to sleep in the cars overnight.

The next day was Christmas Eve, and the students took the time to revise their original plan. It was decided they would break in through a small door into Poets' Corner, close to the chapel. During the day, however, the girl Kay became hypothermic and the group was forced to check her into a hotel.

When the others returned to collect Kay for the night's work, the hotel proprietor became suspicious and called the police. Ian was asked for his driving licence, and the hire car was checked out too. The students were all in a cold sweat, but the officer was satisfied and let them go.

When they reached the abbey, Kay waited in one car for the stone to be brought out, while the men went behind a fence, crossed a builder's yard and reached the side door, prising it open with the crowbar. Inside the chapel, the stone itself proved to be extremely troublesome. As the men hauled it out from beneath the coronation chair, the stone broke into two pieces. The larger piece was placed on Ian's coat, and the men dragged it down the altar steps. Ian carried the smaller piece out to the car, planning to return straightaway to help his friends. As he came out to the fence, he heard Kay bringing the car forward, though this had not been part of the plan. When he went to investigate, she whispered that a policeman was coming.

Ian got into the car, flung a coat over the stone, and put his arms around Kay. The policeman approached the vehicle warily, but relaxed when he saw the amorous young couple. He stopped for a smoke and a chat to pass the time of his shift, while the other men, oblivious to the policeman's presence, cursed Ian and continued to haul the stone closer and closer to the other side of the fence.

Ian could hear his companions struggling with the stone, so in order to divert the officer's attention from them, Kay drove off around the corner into the car park. They stopped by their second vehicle. Ian placed the broken stone in the boot of Kay's car, and asked her to take care of it while he returned to the abbey to help the others lift the bigger stone into the other car.

Kay drove off, but heard a thump, and discovered the boot had not been locked and the stone had rolled out. Despite its weight Kay managed to lift it back in, and made her way out of London to her friend's house in the Midlands. There she left the car and the corner of the stone in a garage, and returned to Scotland by train.

Meanwhile, Ian returned to the abbey to find the stone abandoned with no sign of either his friends or his coat. Exasperated and tired, he had to move it himself. After much trouble, he eventually managed to heave the stone into the car boot. With no idea of where his friends were, he drove around the myriad of tiny streets, feeling exhausted, triumphant and bewildered, and was fortunate enough to find them. Ian and Alan decided to go south to hide the stone, while Gavin travelled north back to Scotland, once again by train.

Having reached Kent, Ian and Alan set about finding a suitable hiding spot for the bulk of the stone. They at last settled on a place, burying it for concealment behind some trees. They took care to note its exact location.

By the time they reached the border, police blocks were in place. As per procedure, they were stopped and questioned, but bluffed their way through. Across the country, the theft had sparked excitement. The police themselves were faced with a huge challenge. Where were they to look? As well as the usual routes of investigation, Scotland Yard also employed water diviners and held séances to try to find the hiding place of the stone.

There was concern that the stone might quickly be damaged by frost, so before he had a chance to recover fully, Ian, along with a new crew, headed back down to Kent to retrieve it. To their dismay, they found Gypsies camped by the hiding place. Ian's friend sounded out one of the men, who warmed to their cause, but warned that there was a stranger in the camp who might not prove as sympathetic. When this man left, the Gypsies willingly helped the group carry the stone back to the car. They removed the front passenger seat, placed the stone in the well, put an old blanket on top of it, and set off again for Scotland. Not far from the border, they stopped for petrol and the attendant, hearing their accents, joked, 'You're not carrying the Stone of Destiny, are you?'

'Aye, it's in the boot!' Ian answered. The attendant laughed, and said that when the police asked, he would tell them the stone had gone through that morning.

Ian later returned to England to retrieve the smaller piece of the stone and on his return, it was hidden away in a factory in a packing case in Bonnybridge. The Stone of Destiny had come home, and many were delighted. But this symbol of Scotland's freedom could not remain shut up and hidden forever.

As the months passed, many Scots were baying for the Stone to be displayed openly in Scotland, where it belonged. But the police were beginning to close in on the students. What was to be done?

A decision was made to leave the repaired Stone of Destiny in a place symbolic of Scottish freedom and independence, Arbroath Abbey. Here, in 1320, the dignitaries of Scotland, supported by Robert the Bruce, declared themselves to the most influential man of the day, the Pope. The Declaration of Arbroath states that 'as long as a hundred of us remain alive, never will we on any conditions be subjected to the lordship of the English. It is in truth not for glory, nor riches, nor honours that we are fighting, but for freedom alone, which no honest man gives up but with life itself.'

The stone did not remain in Arbroath for long. The authorities whipped it back down to Westminster overnight and it stayed there for some years.

In 1996, due to increasing unrest over the border, it was agreed by the English government that it would be a judicial move to return the Coronation Stone to its homeland 'on loan', only to be taken back to England for future coronations.

The students who were involved in the robbery, although questioned, were never charged.

But is the Stone of Destiny the original? Would monks of the day have stood by and allowed an English perpetrator to steal their most valued relic? Would they not have sought to conceal it from English invaders?

For all that the stone has resided in England for hundreds of years and has seen numerous posteriors sat upon it for crowning ceremonies, many doubt that the lump of old red sandstone from Perthshire is the genuine article.

In January 1819 a letter to the *Morning Chronicle* stated that a great stone had been uncovered on the ancient site of Macbeth's castle at Dunsinane. While men had been excavating the area, the ground had given way revealing an underground vault and within it, a large dark stone had been discovered, weighing 250kg and made of some meteoric or semi-metallic material. The article goes on to say that the stone had been sent down to London for tests.

Some say that while the stone was hidden away in 1950 the mason who repaired it actually carved a replica and it was this one that was returned to Westminster.

Today the Stone of Destiny resides in Edinburgh Castle, on display for any who would like to view it, and decide for themselves whether this chiselled rock is indeed the ancient Coronation Stone of the Scottish kings. And whether this actually matters; or is its symbolic value more important?

✧ Chess and Hitchhikers ✧ – an urban myth fae Dundee

One extremely stormy night, when the fire in my grandmother's bedroom was banked up with coal, sending eerie shadows dancing over her heavy antique furniture, she related another tale to me. It concerned a man named Powell, who was a delivery truck driver. On one long, lonely journey he passed through Dundee and picked up a male hitchhiker for company. SB

As the miles passed, the driver and the hitchhiker discussed their favourite hobbies. By coincidence both were chess enthusiasts. The hitchhiker scribbled down his name and address and told Powell to drop by if he was ever passing. It happened to be a town Powell would be visiting in three days' time.

'If I am out,' said the man, 'I'll draw you a chessboard and set you a puzzle and pop it in my tobacco jar. I never forget a promise; the answer will be on the back, but no cheating!'

Three days later Powell turned up at the hitchhiker's door and the man's wife answered. When he explained the reason for his visit, her face turned ashen grey.

'My husband died three days ago,' she said. 'He never returned after a trip to Dundee.' Powell was shocked and explained of his encounter with the woman's husband. He mentioned the drawing that his new acquaintance had promised to make. The woman immediately fetched the tobacco jar. To their utter amazement, there was a rolled up piece of paper in the jar written in her husband's handwriting … a chess puzzle from the man who never forgot a promise.

FIFE

⟡ Dark Tower, Dark Tales ⟡ – Pittenweem's Tolbooth

Pittenweem is a beautiful wee seaside town in Fife, with quaint houses and interesting lanes that climb from the harbour up to the main street. Throngs of people pass through here during the summer months, especially during the Arts Festival in August. Many people open up their homes as miniature galleries; it is a lovely atmosphere.

But there is a darker side to this town. Local author Leonard Low has thoroughly researched this area and its history and has written various books, including The Weem Witch. *The town had been a thriving fishing port, but many contributing factors, including civil war, served to rob it of its working populace and wealth. In those days the church and leading citizens were very influential and in Pittenweem this was not good for the town. In dissolute times, there often has to be a scapegoat to blame for tragic circumstances. Sadly certain people became the focus of the town's grief and they were mainly women. The Tolbooth was the Town Council's chambers but doubled up as a prison; the basement was the dungeon. During the early eighteenth century this building became the centre of torture and death for many who were accused of witchcraft.*

In 2006 Leonard was given permission to give historical tours in the Tolbooth, which had housed a Bren gun during the Second World War but had not been used for jailing purposes since 1790. The walls are raw stone and the narrow winding staircase leads up and up to the roof, which gives a bird's eye view down the coast to Edinburgh.

There is one room on each floor; they are small, dark and damp. Leonard and his friend Greg Stewart (author of Haunted Kirkcaldy*) showed me where the accused would have been chained and described the methods of torture used to extract a confession. Instruments of torture included a 'witch pricker'. This 'tool' had a 10cm shaft, which would be fully punched through the skin anywhere on a person's body. If the victim did not cry out in pain they were condemned as a witch; the area of 'numbness' was referred to as the 'Devil's mark'. The foregone conclusion was that this person must have made a pact with the Devil and the numb area was supposedly where he had touched the person.*

But darker yet are the happenings that have occurred since Leonard began the tours. I met with Leonard and Greg to hear about some of their experiences. GB

A Stabbing Encounter

One time when Leonard had taken a group into the tower, they were on the first floor. He was recounting the tale of Thomas Brown; who was one of the men accused of witchcraft and had been imprisoned in that very room. Suddenly a series of thumps was heard in the room above, then a shout of 'How dare you!' followed by hits and screams. The group all smiled; Leonard must have brought in some actors, but he denied it. Two young men ran up the stone steps to investigate and halted inside the room above; the sound of the hits and skirls could still be heard below. Suddenly the lads turned and fled all the way down the spiral staircase and outside.

Meanwhile, one woman in the remaining group began to scream with fear; as people watched, her jumper was physically being pulled in all directions. Leonard directed everyone back downstairs and out of the tower and examined the pale-faced woman who was visibly shaken. She pulled down her collar and showed a bloody cut that had grazed her neck. She described how two hands had suddenly appeared in front of her and started to stab at her with a knife.

A week or so later Leonard received a message from a man who had been on the same tour. He had not wanted to say anything at the time that might make the group more upset, for nobody else seemed to have seen what he saw. When Leonard had mentioned Thomas Brown, this man had been staring at the doorway of the room and saw another man standing there. This man had spoken and said, 'Lucky Thomas Brown, eh?' Then the onlooker saw the man stalk into the room and attack the woman.

Leonard asked the two young men what they had seen. They described hearing fists smash into someone who seemed to be in the corner of the room. They had seen flurries of dust kicked up as if someone was flailing around trying to avoid blows.

The Bells

Over recent years there have been many unexplained and often unsettling incidents within the Tolbooth. Leonard and Greg describe footsteps and the slamming of wooden doors (where no doors remain) as so common they are not worth recording. Both men underline that they are keen to record genuine material but discount anything that could be termed as manipulative or scare-mongering tactics. Neither make a living out of 'ghost nights'; they respect the place and seek to enhance their understanding of the past and what went on in this building.

From time to time, the two men set up recording devices and leave them in the Tolbooth overnight. One night they had left the tower at 11.50 p.m., having placed recorders and cameras on the ground, first and third floors. When they collected the equipment and listened to the recordings, they were in for a shock.

In the tower there are two bells attached to a clock on an automatic electric timer, which is set to ring out only from 7 a.m. until 7 p.m. The tapes had clearly recorded the two men leaving the tower and departing in their car. About thirty minutes later there was the sound of footsteps followed by the slamming of a wooden door on both the ground and first-floor recorders. But on the third floor, there was the weirdest recording. On it was heard the two men leaving, then the door closing, and immediately after there was the sound of a bell tolling twelve times; this was followed by another twelve rings. After this, the bells began a frenzied ringing, which Leonard described as a 'Hunchback of Notre Dame' routine. It went on for an hour. No bells were heard on the other recorders and there was no neighbourhood disturbance, otherwise there would certainly have been complaints.

I was taken up to see the bells that are in situ today; Leonard rang them. The tone of the bells was completely different to those I heard on the recording.

Greg explained that one torture used in some places was to place a prisoner's head within a bell and then thump it incessantly.

The Murder

Leonard is often asked to go and visit haunted places and has had requests to go on various radio chat shows. Following one interview, he had gone to the Tolbooth and set up tripods at two levels with small cameras that look like torches. He set them to run for as long as the battery lasted and journeyed back down to his home in London, where he was living at the time.

While working the next day, he felt a strange prickling sensation over his head. He left his work and at that moment his phone rang. It was a school acquaintance Leonard had not seen for 35 years. The man explained that he and his mother had heard the radio interview the day before, and his mother thought that she could help Leonard. Leonard was always open to people widening his understanding of the Tolbooth and its previous occupants and agreed to speak with the lady. She was in her eighties and had been chair-bound for some years. She was very self-effacing but told Leonard that she was a transient medium; she could visit the tower and maybe help him understand things a bit better. She then proceeded to 'enter' the tower while seated in her chair in her own living room.

The lady described in detail the number of steps that lead up to the Tolbooth's first floor and spoke of the plastered door and cupboard that are there. She then 'walked' up the stairs to the next floor, entered the room and apologised; she had knocked over a torch on a tripod that she presumed Leonard had placed there.

She went back out to the stairwell and climbed up to the next floor and there she began to recount a story of two girls who had been imprisoned in the room. A minister had come and taken one away from the tower. The following day the same man had returned and strangled the other, a young lass called Isobel Adam who was perhaps 10 years old. She was wearing a red dress and had long red hair. The man took Isobel's body and hid it in the plastered-up cupboard two floors below.

This corroborates a recording that Leonard has in which a voice declares herself to be Isobel Adam and when asked if she is trapped, her young voice pleads for help.[5] Leonard was also aware that over the years there have been a number of independent sightings of a young girl with long red hair in the tower.

---

5 A strange phenomenon that both Greg and Leonard have discovered is that when they have made recordings and asked questions of previous occupants, they may feel a coldness in the room but although their ears have not picked up any sounds, the tape has recorded voices, as in the case of Isobel Adam. In another case like this, Greg and his son found their tape had recorded a man called William, who apparently was not a prisoner, but may well have been involved in the witch persecutions. He was asked, do you object to people being brought into the tower? His voice answered, 'There is too much talking!' The two were alone in the dark tower, but following this interaction, a stone missile came out of nowhere and hit Greg's son in the chest. It turned out to be a bit of glass, a material that was not used in the building of this tower of torture.

Leonard advertises his tours as a historical session where visitors can experience the prison as it was so many years ago. He does not tell them about the unexplained occurrences that some have had. There can be months when the tower seems quiet and empty, but at other times there can be a run of sightings and sounds that leave Leonard in no doubt that Pittenweem Tolbooth still harbours a dark and violent past that somehow makes itself known today.

✧ Influence from the Other Side ✧ – true tales fae St Andrew's

St Andrew's in Fife has existed from ancient times; it is a delightful university town. The first account written here I heard from a camper I met on Tiree. The second story I received from my Aunt, Isobel Maguire. GB

Superstitious Actions

As you walk along North Street in St Andrew's, you will see outside St Salvator's Chapel and Sallies Quad that the initials 'P.H.' are embedded in the cobbled road. This plaque commemorates a man called Patrick Hamilton.

Patrick Hamilton lived in the sixteenth century and came as a young abbot to the University at St Andrew's, which was the capital of the Scottish Church and of learning. The Church at this time was Roman Catholic, but while training in France, Patrick had been influenced by alternative ways of religious thinking. He was eager to share these doctrines in his preaching but under threat of arrest and trial he fled to Germany. Yet Patrick was so convinced by his beliefs he chose to return to St Andrew's a few months later. He openly preached his views and rather than arrest him, the Archbishop, David Beaton, invited him to share his convictions at a conference, which Hamilton did for a month. He clearly knew he was signing his own death warrant, by providing the opposition with ammunition against him, yet nevertheless he seized the opportunity to speak the truth as he now saw it.

He was summoned and condemned as a heretic on thirteen charges. Although a reprieve from death was promised, it was overridden. To prevent an attempt at a rescue by Hamilton's influential friends, he was burnt at the stake the very same day. His final words were, 'Lord Jesus, receive my spirit.' The fire that burnt Hamilton to death continued from midday until six o'clock at night.

Hamilton's bravery and convictions in the face of death influenced many and acted as a major catalyst to the whole Protestant movement; he was the first martyr of the cause. The initials 'P.H.' indicate the site of Hamilton's pyre.

If you are in St Andrew's and are walking along North Street you may notice that if students are walking along the cobbled road, they suddenly give this particular spot a wide body-swerve; for it is a firmly held belief that if you stand on Patrick Hamilton's initials you will fail your exams! Apparently two remedies are available. You can remove the curse by taking part in the May dip or by circling the light at the end of the pier three times!

It is said that another peculiar happening occurred at the time of Hamilton's burning; the outline of a face appeared on the chapel wall. Today if you peer up at the wall you can still see a stone that is said to have peculiar markings in the shape of Patrick Hamilton's face.

A Caring Spirit

Isobel and her twin sister Marion used to go and stay with relatives in Airlie and now and again a minister and his wife from St Andrew's would visit; the couple were very fond of the twins. The minister had the experience recorded here.

The minister had been ill for some time. For weeks he had not risen from bed. He was usually sprightly, bouncing with good health and bonhomie, but bronchitis had hit him hard and his family were concerned that he was not making any improvement.

One day when the rest of the family were out, there came a knock on his bedroom door. Knowing he was alone in the house, the minister sighed and with great difficulty struggled to rise from the bed. His limbs were weak and wobbly from lack of use and he felt light-headed. He clutched bedroom furniture for support, and felt very breathless. It took a long time to reach the door, but eventually the minister reached it and turned the handle, cautiously pulling it open.

A tall man was standing there wearing a fine, Inverness tweed cape. His high-crowned black hat was set at a jaunty angle and he was leaning on his shiny cane. The man had pleasing features and a good head of white hair framed his face. He smiled warmly at the minister, bowed graciously towards him, touched his hand to his hat and disappeared.

The invalid stood there, bewildered and shaky from exertion, but not in the least bit frightened.

When his wife returned later, she was delighted to find her husband sitting up in bed, looking brighter; the sick lassitude seemed to have gone. This was such a relief. The minister told his wife about his strange encounter; she did not know what to make of it but was pleased to see her husband chatting. Although he was still weak, he seemed much more like his old self.

From the day of the encounter, the minister's health returned slowly; he had definitely turned a corner.

The strange visitor came one more time to visit the minister, when he was alone in the house. Again there was a knock on his bedroom door, but this time the minister was able to get up and reach the door much more quickly and with far less discomfort. His visitor beamed warmly at the minister and then left, vanishing before his eyes.

The minister was curious; why was this man coming to visit him and who was he?

One icy morning some months later, the minister had regained his full strength and was walking through town when the heavens opened and it began to pour with rain. He was just outside the door of the Harris' home. This house belonged to two elderly spinster sisters who were regular churchgoers at the minister's church. He knocked briskly and was ushered in. Fussily the ladies took the minister's coat and hat and insisted he have a cup of tea and a warm by the fire. Soon the three were in lively discussion and the conversation turned to local ghosts.

The minister was reminded of his own experience and shared it with the two ladies. Nodding, one of them took down an old photograph album from a shelf. She opened it and leafed through until she came to a certain page. She handed the minister the album, smiling knowingly. The minister looked at the black and white photograph. Looking up at him was a friendly face he recognised, even down to the cloak and hat. The minister was astonished and the sisters laughed out loud to see his surprise. They told him that his experience was not unusual. Apparently the gentleman had previously lived in the house where the minister now stayed and he had also been a minister. His name was John Ingles and the two sisters said their father had always spoken of the man very highly as the kindest he had ever known. It was not the first time Mr Ingles had graciously come to visit his old home to make sure all was well with the occupants!

The minister never saw his visitor again, but he always thought that this gentleman was to be thanked for his unusual and speedy recovery.

STIRLINGSHIRE

✧ Rogue and Reiver ✧ – the legends o' Rob Roy MacGregor fae Balquhidder

What convoluted and conflicting tales are told of this man! A powerful, daunting character emerges through the many myths and stories. I have been aware of Rob Roy from childhood; we passed Kirkintilloch Rob Roy FC frequently on our way to church. I vaguely connected the man with the southwest highlands and found it strange to see a statue of him on a rock above a burn on the outskirts of Peterculter outside Aberdeen! To paint an accurate picture of this colourful figure may be hard, when so many stories were passed on orally and are now only preserved in written form, but here I try to tell the story of Rob Roy, how circumstances and politics shaped and developed the man. GB

Rob Roy was born in 1671 at a time when the crowning of William the usurper and the Act of Union in 1707 would soon have Scotland in turmoil. While Rob Roy was still living, a publication appeared in 1723, called 'The Highland Rogue, or the Memorable Actions of the Celebrated Robert MacGregor commonly called Rob Roy, digested from the Memorandum of an Authentick Scotch Manuscript.' He was a legend even before he had died!

This man was the second son of MacGregor, laird of Glengyle and as such would not inherit, which led him to become a resourceful man, seeking to make his living through the family-held tradition of cattle reiving. Rob Roy had a kind and roguish disposition; he was adventurous, brave, tall and broad and had unusually long arms. He was not a man with whom to pick a sword fight!

For a variety of reasons Rob Roy's father had been captured, chiefly for his cattle stealing. For Rob Roy to help his father gain his freedom, he had to instigate a 'police' force, the Glengyle Watch, which would ensure cattle remained on the land where they belonged and law and order would be enforced. Rob Roy managed this well and turned it into a flourishing business.

The very first call for the Watch came from none other than the factor of Breadalbane. In the night fifteen head of cattle had been stolen while grazing at Finlarig. Rob Roy gathered a dozen men together; the Watch had some difficulty following the reivers, the Macraes of Kintail, but eventually Rob Roy tracked them down. During the night the sleepy robbers were woken by the chaos of panicking beasts and were assailed by what seemed a great multitude of men. Most deserted, leaving two dead and a handful of wounded men. The Watch were richly rewarded for the safe return of the beasts to Finlarig.

By the time he died, Rob Roy's father had already bequeathed Rob Roy a farm in Balquhidder where his cattle herd became established. Rob Roy's older brother inherited the estate on their father' death, but he did not live long, and Rob Roy became chieftain of the clan until his nephew came of age.

Over time, in order to put a more respectable name to his business, Rob Roy persuaded many local landowners to pay him and his men a regular advanced fee to protect their cows from other reivers and if the cattle were stolen, Rob Roy would be obliged to find or replace them. With his wily ways, his knowledge of the hills and the ways of droving, Rob Roy rarely came up empty-handed.

The lords of the land often took a dismal view of MacGregor's occupation and from time to time there were clashes with authority.

Rob Roy was pursued, sometimes captured, but proved as slippery as an eel, even when closely guarded! He often managed to negotiate his freedom to live the life he intended without interference.

After a time, being an astute businessman, Rob Roy sought to align himself with a man of prominence, where their mutual partnership would be convenient and beneficial to both. Thus in 1703 he approached James, fourth Marquis of Montrose, who saw agreeable business possibilities in Rob Roy supporting his trade in kyloe cattle. For years this worked well for both; Rob Roy was an effective factor, always procuring finances or cattle when required.

But in 1708, on the back of the first Jacobite uprising, Rob Roy had been distracted from his cattle duty for Montrose and had to entrust the moving of a particular herd to a drover by the name of Macdonald. Unfortunately, the beasts vanished and Montrose unequivocally regarded Rob Roy as the culprit, demanding full recompense, which Rob Roy was at a loss to fulfil. Their partnership was broken and a long enmity was born between the two strong-willed men.

By October 1712, Montrose declared Rob Roy a vagabond and a villain, having vanished with £1,000 sterling as well as cattle. A manhunt began, involving many, including a man called Killearn, who was Montrose's man. Killearn was also Sheriff Deputy for the County of Stirling, and as punishment to Rob Roy he was given possession of Rob Roy's home at Inversnaid.

When Killearn and his posse arrived at Inversnaid, Rob Roy's wife Mary was still present. When she discovered that she was to be dispossessed, Mary was determined to retrieve at least some of her own articles. Sadly, this delay proved too much temptation for the invaders. Many hours later when the men had finished with her, Mary stumbled out of her home, a broken woman. Her clothes were in tatters and she would not speak of the horrors she had endured at the hands of Killearn and his men. For many years, she remained isolated living away from her husband, nursing her burning hate and pain.

For Rob Roy life was grim; he was estranged from his family, he was bankrupt and on the run with no place to call home. But many men still looked to him for leadership and depended on him for survival.

As Killearn was now the factor collecting rents for Montrose, Rob Roy lost no opportunity to provoke and harry his wife's abuser. On one instance Rob Roy was able to kidnap Killearn offering his wife the opportunity for revenge. She refused and no harm came to the factor, but he was badly shaken at the potential punishment that might have been inflicted. The only loss was to Montrose; his November rents were appropriated and well used by Rob Roy and his men.

By 1715, Scotland was divided; some supported the new Hanoverian king, George, while others, the Jacobites, were loyal to James. Rob Roy chose to fight under the Earl of Mar, to see the Stuart king restored to the Scottish throne. From being a harried outlaw, Rob Roy was now a respected soldier in uniform with authority; being a man who knew the land, he was strategic to the success of the army. This must have put a spring back into Rob Roy's step!

But the Battle of Sheriffmuir in 1715 was a disaster for the Stuart followers and not long after this Rob Roy sought new patronage; aligning himself with the fallen-out-of-grace Argyll. This led some to believe that Rob Roy was actually spying for Argyll during the rebellion.

The loyalty Rob Roy showed for Argyll was rewarded with a secure home. He was reunited with his family under Argyll's protection, and was content for some time. But political pressure continued to haunt this man of the mountains. Attempts were made to blackmail Rob Roy into betraying his lord, which he refused to do. It was decided that if MacGregor would not willingly betray Argyll, then he would be forced to by devious means, or else suffer captivity.

The gnawing desire to capture Rob Roy was two-fold. It would be a relief for everyone to have this thieving outlaw put away for good but, more importantly, he was the one with power to lay charges at John Roy (Argyll), which he refused to do.

Although Rob Roy was pleased to be living on protected land, he longed to return home to Balquhidder to continue his cattle business. During the year of Jubilee, he requested that he might take possession of a croft that was vacant in the glen. The request was brought to Atholl, who saw an opportunity to trick his adversary. A letter was sent requesting Rob Roy's presence at Atholl's residence, with the promise of safe passage, but signed by Atholl's brother, not himself.

With alacrity, Rob Roy took up the invitation and willingly travelled to the duke's home. He was welcomed warmly, but not invited into the house; instead Atholl suggested they take a turn about his beautiful gardens. Rob Roy did not suspect treachery, even when he was requested to remove his sword and dagger, supposedly at the behest of the duchess. He was not even offered a drink to slake his thirst. This lack of hospitality was suspicious, but Rob Roy said nothing as he and Atholl walked and talked. But to Rob Roy's dismay, Atholl insisted he betray his patron in return for the restoration of his land and freedom. Unwilling to play any part in blackening Argyll as a Jacobite, Rob Roy found himself arrested and despite the promise of safe conduct, Rob Roy was unable to defend himself and was hustled off to jail.

Atholl felt triumphant and bragged about his duping of the rogue. It did not take Rob Roy long to escape, yet not without mishap for he was grazed in the thigh by a musket ball. Unable to make his way directly home due to the hue and cry, his leg suffered and the wound was festering by the time he reached his Mary and clean bandages. It took time, but he recovered well.

Some time later, Graham Killearn devised a fail-safe plan for the capture of Rob Roy. Soldiers had been placed at either end of Balquhidder Glen, effectively trapping Rob Roy. The next day another posse would march over the hills and into the glen to flush their quarry out of one of his favourite haunts at Portanellen.

The night before the attack, Killearn and Donald Stewart, who commanded one of the detachments, were seated in a cave overlooking Loch Katrine. They were both enjoying their repast, anticipating the morrow's conquest, when they heard movement in the darkness at the rear of the cave. It was none other than Rob Roy. He enjoyed their discomfort but allowed the men to leave unharmed, if very humiliated!

The conflict with Montrose carried on; one would rob the other and vice versa, until, after ten years, the conflict was more out of habit than bad feeling. Rob Roy, with hat in hand, asked for the penalty to be removed from over his head for being an outlaw. A bargain was struck - Montrose would now own the MacGregor land, of which Rob Roy had been dispossessed anyway, and have the title of duke to his name and Rob Roy would walk out a free man. From then on, Rob Roy was able to live peaceably, in his own home, no longer living under the shadow of possible, sudden arrest.

But never a man to live quietly, Rob Roy had his eye on property that was not his own. He brought a mob of one hundred MacGregors to take possession of a farm near Balquhidder, which rightfully belonged to a John McLaren. Indignant at Rob Roy's tactics, McLaren managed to enlist help; his men outnumbered Rob Roy's two to one. The two sides were drawn up, swords unsheathed and ready to do battle.

Rob Roy, with the wisdom of years, saw things could go unnecessarily badly for his men and produced a white flag of truce. This was accepted, but the McLaren supporters heckled and mocked Rob Roy and his men. Seeing the need to boost morale and allow a release for adrenalin-laden warriors, Rob Roy suggested one-to-one combat between himself and one of the opposition. A lad, many years Rob Roy's junior, volunteered and the pair set to with swords. The MacGregors prepared to settle back and enjoy watching the young upstart be coolly licked by their esteemed leader, but they were dismayed to see Rob Roy intent on hot-headed dashes at his opponent. With sudden clarity, realisation dawned on his men; Rob Roy's sight was failing and he was doing all he could to prevent the other's sword from coming near his person. Rob Roy was the first to be wounded and good-naturedly he congratulated the lad on his triumph, but swore never to raise his sword again.

Although Rob Roy had consistently clashed with authority and evaded many captures over the years, his final days were quiet ones. It was in 1734 and the great man lay sick in bed while Mary watched her listless husband weaken. It must have been hard to bear. But word came that an old enemy of Rob's was on his way to visit him in his sick bed. On hearing this, Rob's lassitude seemed to fall away and clear-eyed he demanded his nurse to dress him and seat him with his sword in hand and musket by his side. He had no strength left in his great unresponsive frame to aid his poor wife. But Mary had Rob Roy ready and waiting before the visitor arrived to gloat over his adversary. What was the man's surprise when he saw not a defeated and withered invalid but rather a foe unchanged? Rob Roy's burning gaze and glint of a smile dashed the intruder's hopes to finally have one over on his tormentor of years! Hurriedly, the visitor muttered a few words to Rob Roy but he could not get out of the house quick enough! The moment the man fled, Rob Roy almost collapsed where he sat, his sword clattering to the floor. The effort had been too much and Rob Roy never rose from his bed again.

As I have travelled through the Highlands where Rob Roy and his men herded cattle and disappeared from pursuit, often melting into the heather, my respect has grown for this man who was such a legend. Although a rogue he was a simple man at heart, whose business head caused him to clash with the politically powerful of the day. He was a man who could never belong to towns and cities, yet was perfectly at home in the wilds of hill and glen, thinking nothing of a seventy-mile trip to rescue cattle!

Rob Roy's grave is near the place he called home, Kirkton of Balquhidder, and his wife Mary is buried alongside him.

✧ House to Let ✧ – an urban myth fae Denny

My grandmother told me one story that she had read in the papers and it has stayed with me. It was the tale of an escaped lunatic from Denny in Stirlingshire. A dangerous man had escaped from a local asylum, where he had been interned for murdering his mother with an axe. She had been a frail and gentle old woman who had no means of protecting herself from her violent, insane son. SB

One day a young couple arrived at the local estate agent just as he was closing up his shop. They were new to the area and looking for a reasonably priced home to buy. Most of the properties in the town were outwith their budget, but there was one cottage which, although a bit isolated and out of town, was cheaper than the rest. They were eager to view the property, and reluctantly the estate agent gave them the key; he warned them that as it was dusk and the electricity was off, they would see very little. They agreed they would go and see the premises briefly that night and return in the morning to meet the agent for a proper viewing.

In the gathering gloom the couple drove quickly out to see the cottage, but lost their way twice. By the time they arrived it was very dark, but the husband had a torch, and leaving his wife in the car he made his way up to the cottage. The 'For Sale' sign was clearly visible in the window. He unlocked the door and stepped into the house, but immediately a figure lunged and struck him forcefully with a spade; the man was decapitated instantly.

The escaped psychopath lifted his gory prize and carried the head down to the car, where the unsuspecting wife was waiting. Laughing, he held the head up by the hair, as the wife's screams echoed along the glen. Fortunately at that moment the police arrived. They had been alerted by the prison. Concerns had been raised that the psychopath might revisit the scene of his first murder; the cottage was the killer's family home.

EDINBURGH

✧ Cannibals on the Royal Mile ✧

No visit to Scotland is complete without a visit to Parliament. At the foot of the Royal Mile in Edinburgh is Holyrood House, the home of the Scottish Parliament, and incorporated into it is a red-roofed seventeenth-century building called Queensberry House. Nowadays it houses offices for the presiding officer of the Parliament, along with two deputy presiding officers, the Parliament's chief executive and other staff members. It was once owned by James Douglas, the second Duke of Queensberry, who was one of the driving forces behind the 1707 Treaty of the Union. SB

In 1707 angry crowds of demonstrators had gathered in Parliament Square to protest against the Union. James Douglas went to try to calm down the situation and his servants and family had gone with him, but two people remained behind.

The Earl of Drumlanrig had not gone for he was the Duke's lunatic son, and was usually securely locked in his room. And in the kitchen one little servant boy had been left turning the roast pig on the spit for dinner.

Unfortunately, with all the excitement and panic caused by the near rioting in the streets, the door of the lunatic's bedroom had been left unlocked. When the household returned, it was to a scene of carnage and horror. The earl had wandered down to the kitchen and found food. He had removed the pig from the spit and skewered the boy in its place. He was found to be contentedly eating the child by the hearth. The oven can still be seen in the Parliament's Allowances Office today. Not surprisingly it is said that the murdered kitchen boy still haunts Queensberry House; the stench of roasting flesh can occasionally be smelt wafting through the corridor, the victim of Scotland's very own Hannibal Lecter.

✧ Nine of Diamonds ✧

One of the most infamous men to walk the streets of Edinburgh was John Dalrymple, Secretary of State and Master of Stair. SB

John Dalrymple was the man who passed on the orders giving permission for the annihilation of the Macdonald clan in 1692. Legend claims the Secretary of State wrote 'Kill them all' on a nine of diamonds card. The layout of this particular card is said to resemble the Dalrymple crest of arms. From that day, the nine of diamonds has been called the curse of Scotland as it instigated the shameful Glen Coe Massacre.

✧ The Ballad o' Binnorie ✧

Several versions of 'Binnorie' are placed near Edinburgh. The myth of speaking bones is international, used by Shamans everywhere. 'Binnorie' or 'The Twa Sisters' is No. 10 in Francis J. Child's The English and Scottish Popular Ballads. *In the song the second and fourth lines are repeated refrains, which occur in each verse; the second line being 'Binnorie, o' Binorrie' and the fourth being 'By the bonnie mill dams o' Binnorie'. In order for the reader to read the story the refrains have been removed. The translation of some of the Scots is in brackets beside each line. SB*

There were twa sisters sat in a boouer (bower)
There cam a knight tae be their wooer.

He's coorted the eldest with glove and ring,
But he's lovit the youngest abeen aathing. (above everything)

He's coorted the eldest with brooch and knife,
But he's lovit the youngest a mair than his life.

The eldest she wis vexèd sair, (very upset)
And sairit be the sister fair. (woe be to)

It was upon a mornin clear,
She cried untae her sister dear.

'Noo sister, sister come tak me by the hand,
And we'll walk doun be the water strand.'

The youngest she stood upon a stane,
The eldest she cam and she shovit her in.

'Noo sister, sister come gie tae me yer hand,
And ye sall be heir tae aa my land.

'Ill faa the land that I should tak,
For ye twinèd me fae my loves back.

'For yer cherry cheeks and yer yaller hair,
Gar me gae a maiden for ever mair.' (forced)

Sometimes she sunk, sometimes she swam,
Till she floated doun tae the miller's dam.

'Miller, miller come draw yer dam,
There's either a mermaid or a milk-white swan.'

The miller he hastened and drew his dam,
And there he's fund a droonèd woman,

Ye quidna see her little, wee feet, (you could not)
Her gowden tresses they were sae deep. (her hair was so long)

Ye quidna see her middle sae sma,
Her gowden girdle it wis sae braw. (golden belt)

Ye quidna see her fingers sae sma,
Wi diamond rings they were coverèd aa.

An aa amon her yella hair, (all among)
A rope o' pearls wis twinèd there.

By and cam a harper fine, (came by)
That harpèd for the king tae dine.

He's made a harp ootan her breast bane, (out of her breast bone)
Fa soun would melt a hert o' stane. (whose sound)

He's taen three strands o' her yella hair, (taken)
And wi them strung this harp sae fair.

He's gane untae her faither's haa, (gone to … hall)
And there wis the court assemblit aa.

He's lain the harp doun on a stane,
And syne it began tae play its lane. (then … by itself)

'Yonder sits my faither the king,
And yonder sits my mither the queen.'

'Yonder stands my brither Hugh,
And by him my William sweet and true.'

But the last tune that the harp played then,
Was, 'Waes tae ma sister, false Helen.' (woe)

✧ The Golden Screw ✧ – an urban myth o' aliens

A strange tale circulates among the Scottish travellers, which is based on the child's urban myth of the bellybutton! It is about alien–human interaction, a version of which was told to me by the traveller, Stanley Robertson. Here is my version, which concludes in Edinburgh. SB

A spaceship was hovering over Scotland, hoping to transfer an alien in human guise onto Earth to gather information on how humans spent their time. The aliens had managed to replicate a covering suit that felt like human skin, but to draw it together, a small screw was required where the umbilical would have been. This was no bigger than a pinhead, but the alien metal was so luminous that if uncovered it sent out an intense ray, instantly drawing attention to the tiny screw.

It was a particularly hot summer month in Scotland, and having observed the Scots' behaviour in the heat, the alien was dressed appropriately in shorts and T-shirt. He had been transported to Inverness first, and had joined a tour of Loch Ness on *The Nessie Hunter*, along with eleven other passengers. The alien sat in the bow of the boat, looking out towards Urquhart Castle. He was recording a very interesting commentary about the loch into a tiny device fitted into his left earlobe. Because his vision was adapted with radar, he could distinctly see the Loch Ness Monster swimming in the water about 20 fathoms beneath the boat. He began to jump up and down, waving his arms excitedly, but as he did so his T-shirt rode up, and unfortunately, everyone on the boat began to laugh and point at him. There was a dazzling beam emerging from his midriff, which all the tourists began to film. Crestfallen, the alien went and hid in a toilet, and stayed there until the cruise boat landed.

Aberdeen was the next city for the alien to explore. While strolling on the beach, he was drawn to the music of Codonas, the local fairground. The top attraction there was the Aberdeen Eye, with twenty gondolas holding four people each. It rose up to 100 feet in the air, overlooking the beach and the North Sea. It was very hot indeed, so hot that the alien lifted his T-shirt a little to catch the breeze. Unfortunately, as he did so, the tiny screw emitted such a powerful beam of light that planes trying to land at the airport, and ships coming into harbour, misread their navigational instructions, and a state of emergency was declared in the city. The alien was very lucky for he managed to slip away in the general commotion.

Next day, he travelled to Dundee, and booked himself onto a zombie session at Battlefield Live Dundee. He was handed a modern laser tag, for a close-quarters combat experience with special sound effects and lighting. After a while the alien grew bored and hot, as his synthetic human skin did not allow him to sweat. He removed his T-shirt and stuffed it into his backpack. Of course, the instant he did this, the dazzling rays blinded the staff zombies who quickly called security and had him thrown out onto the street.

Glasgow was the next great Scottish city the alien visited. Crowds appeared to be heading towards Ibrox football stadium, which had four stands. Football was not something with which the alien was familiar on his planet, which was many light-years away from Earth. Two teams of people were running back and forth on the pitch, wearing blue or green jerseys, and depending on where the ball was going, there was tremendous shouting. Not wishing to be unsociable, when the humans around him leapt up and down, the alien copied them. Inevitably, his T-shirt hiked up and the blinding strobe of light from the tiny screw took everyone's focus off the game. There was much booing and hissing, and he was hustled from the stadium and warned not to return.

The alien had almost decided to give up on Scotland, but there was one city that he had not visited, Edinburgh, the capital city of the country. While walking down the Royal Mile from Edinburgh Castle to the Palace of Holyrood House he saw people entering a tall building with a crowning spire.

'Why are people going in there?' he asked a passer-by.

'Why, that's St Giles Cathedral, it is a church. Folk go in there to ask God to grant them their wishes.'

The alien stepped inside the cool cathedral, but could not see a god anywhere, whatever 'a god' was. But the passer-by's response had given him an idea. Telepathically, he contacted his mother ship, and asked his commander how the tiny gold screw could be removed. The instructions were quite specific. He had to walk to the top of the hill of Arthur's Seat at midnight, lie down flat and face the night sky.

The alien could hardly contain his excitement. With midnight approaching, he toiled up the hill, and lay down at the very top looking up at the stars. One star glowed brighter than the rest; it was the mother ship, and swiftly it approached and hovered above the alien. A door slid open and a ray of light, glowing orange and white, shone down on the alien where he lay. An object appeared travelling along the beam; it was a golden screwdriver. When it reached the alien, he took it with trembling hands and began to unwind the tiny gold screw.

Carefully, carefully, he turned it, until it was slack enough to remove by hand. Triumphantly, he took it out and stood up. And then his bum fell off.

✧ A Well Kent Dug ✧ – the legend o' Greyfriars Bobby

My grandmother's most 'child friendly' tale was Greyfriars Bobby, the loyal dog which stayed by its master's grave until its own demise. That always reduced me to tears, almost (but not quite) as effectively as Black Beauty. My grandmother would be spinning in her grave to read how matters concerning Bobby sit now. SB

Once upon a time, most visitors to Edinburgh visited the statue of Greyfriars Bobby; nowadays, they gather there to set off on the Harry Potter Trail. They may have heard the recent theory reported in the *Daily Mail* in August 2011, that Greyfriars Bobby was an urban myth invented to attract tourists. The report gave the evidence as coming from Dr Jan Bondeson who wrote the book *Greyfriars Bobby: The Most Faithful Dog in the World*. Dr Bondeson said, 'I knew the famous story of Greyfriar's Bobby but the more I researched it the more I smelt a rat.' Apparently there were *two* Bobbies from 1858 to 1872, neither of whom were owned by the deceased man beside whose grave they sat.

Bondeson discovered that one dog was a stray, which had trotted into Heriot's hospital and was then removed to the graveyard. The curator of the cemetery, James Brown, began to look after the dog and the locals presumed it was mourning its dead master. News spread and visitors flooded to the churchyard to see 'Bobby', and due to the British love for dogs many people donated money to Mr Brown for the dog's upkeep. Many visitors would then pop into the local restaurant for something to eat, which pleased the owner, John Traill.

When the first 'Bobby' died in 1867, Mr Brown and Mr Traill replaced it with another, which kept visitors' interest in the area and made sure they spent their money locally!

Dr Bondeson was quoted as saying: 'Pictures of the dog known as Greyfriars Bobby show a distinct change in May or June 1867.

The first was an elderly, tired dog who was not much to look at, while the second was a lively terrier that ran around and fought other dogs.'

This discovery explains Bobby's longevity; he was supposed to have lived for 18 years; 10 to 12 years is a good life-span for a Skye terrier. Bondeson declared, 'In my opinion, all the theories about the dog's life are about as full of holes as a piece of Swiss cheese.'

There were mutterings about the story of Greyfriars Bobby from various Edinburgh locals 'in the know' and many newspaper writers tried to pour doubt on the legend – but Bobby has vanquished them all, for you can imagine the indignant reaction to the newspaper report about this great Scottish icon!

✧ Jekyll and Hyde ✧ – the true tale o' William Brodie

William Brodie lived from 1741 to 1788 and was more commonly known as Deacon Brodie. He was a cabinetmaker, a deacon of a trade's guild and an Edinburgh city councillor. SB

William Brodie's 'day' jobs were decent and respectable. By night, however, he was a burglar, who thieved partly to pay for the thrill of it and partly to pay off his gambling debts. With the addition of certain nefarious activities he was able to look after his two mistresses and five children. During the day he repaired locks and by night he picked them. He had been a juryman and was a member of the Edinburgh Cape Club; he rubbed shoulders with Robert Burns and Sir Henry Raeburn.

In 1786 Brodie masterminded an armed raid on an Excise Office, for which he enlisted the help of three experienced robbers, Ainslie, Brown and Smith, but it went badly wrong. Ainslie was captured and betrayed his fellows to escape punishment. When Brodie entered court for his trial he was wearing a blue coat, a flowery waistcoat and white satin breeches with white silk stockings. Sporting a cocked hat and a powdered wig he sat calmly throughout. He complained that during his imprisonment his toe- and fingernails had grown longer than those of Nebuchadnezzar, indeed longer than those of a mandarin.

In 1788 Brodie and Smith were found guilty and hanged on a gallows that Brodie had designed and paid for himself the preceding year. 'What is hanging?' Brodie asked on the gallows. 'A leap in the dark!'

On the day of his hanging, it was said that Brodie wore a steel collar to prevent the noose from strangling him. It was believed that Brodie bribed the hangman to arrange for his body to be caught under the trapdoor and revived after the hanging. If so, it did not succeed; he was buried in an unmarked grave in Buccleuch church in Chapel Street, which is now a city car park.

Robert Louis Stevenson's father had hired Brodie to make furniture for him; the man apparently inspired Stevenson to create the character of Jekyll and Hyde.

LOTHIAN

✧ A Close Shave ✧
– an urban myth fae North Berwick

Traffic patrol officers from North Berwick were involved in an unsettling incident whilst checking for speeding motorists on the road between Oldhamstocks and Grantshouse. SB

Two officers were using a hand-held radar device to trap unwary motorists on the Edinburgh to London A1 road. One of the officers was astonished to find that his target had registered a speed of over 300 miles per hour. The £5,000 machine then seized up and could not be reset by the bewildered officers. The radar had in fact latched on to a NATO Tornado aircraft flying over the North Sea. It had been taking part in a simulated low-flying exercise over the Borders and southern Scotland. Although the police had refused to comment, the officers were advised to point their radar guns inland in future.

THE BORDERS

✧ One Good Turn ✧

There has been a fort on the site of Thirlestane Castle in the Borders for many centuries, defending Edinburgh and the north from the south. Here lived John Maitland, Earl of Lauderdale, who was a faithful follower of King Charles II, and who after some turbulent years was appointed Secretary of State for Scotland. In the midst of political intrigue this story is a delightful insight into domestic life. At least some of it is true; I leave you to decide how much! GB

It had been another harsh spring with little respite from cold winds and snow and for the Hardies up on Tollus Hill it had meant a poor lambing season. It was now May and the six-month rent at Whitsun was due in the next few days.

Tam's face was tight with worry as he ate his porridge.

'I'll away up and see how the twin lambs are farin wioot their ain mother.'

Maggie got up from the table and put her small strong arms about her husband.

'Tam we will get by, I ken it.' Her voice was soft, but her words were determined. Tam smiled and stood up. He kissed his wee wife on her forehead and taking his old coat from its hook, he went out to do his morning chores. Maggie's jaw clenched as she tried to think what she could do about the due rent.

Some hours later there was a steady knock on the great door of Thirlestane Castle and when the head servant opened the door he smiled.

'Maggie Hardie, it's grand to see you!'

'G'd day Mr McHardy, is the earl in?'

McHardy had known Maggie from when she was a wee lass; her mother had been the cook in the castle. Maggie had not changed that much and the man knew that stubborn look. McHardy showed Maggie into a room and before long the earl appeared.

'Maggie!' he smiled. 'How can I help you the day?'

Maggie nodded and curtsied and said, 'Earl I have come wi a request for you.'

The earl nodded and listened as Maggie told him of the harsh winter and cruel spring that had robbed the Hardies of their livelihood.

'So,' Maggie concluded, 'we hivna the money to pay the rent yet sir, but we will soon, I promise. We dinna want to leave Tollus, it's oor hame and we love it!'

The earl was silent for a moment, then he looked stern.

'Maggie you are telling me there is still snaw on the hill at the end o' May?'

'Aye sir! You widna believe it doon in the valley, it's so wairm here!'

'Well I will make a bargain wi you Maggie.'

The young woman sat up, her eyes expectant.

'If by the middle o' July you can show me that there are three snawballs still on the hill, then I will forgo your rent this term.'

Maggie's face flushed with relief and her eyes sparkled, 'Aye sir, it's a bargain thank you.' She shook his hand and left. As soon as she had climbed up the hill Maggie went over to the north side, to the coldest rock formation where the sun rarely reached. The snow was still lying thick here, and Maggie began to fashion snowballs like pure white eggs. Then carefully she placed them under the deepest, darkest rock.

In July on a very hot day Maggie returned to the castle to see the earl, who remarked, 'Well Maggie, I cannot see any snowballs!'

Maggie replied tartly, 'Well sir the temperature difference between the mild valley floor and Tollus Hill would have meant I was carrying water to the castle, not snowballs! You will have to climb the hill to see that I have kept my side of the bargain.'

By the time the earl returned to Thirlestane, his respect for the Hardies had deepened; it was a tough existence on the hill. He smiled as he recalled Maggie's triumphant flourish as she had produced ten snowballs from underneath a rocky ledge. The earl had told her there and then, that no more rent would be expected for the next year and a half as she had produced over three times the amount agreed. He had turned away so that he did not embarrass the woman, as grateful tears slid down her cold cheeks.

Maggie never forgot her master's generosity, and some years later when he was incarcerated in prison in London on the order of Cromwell she was able to help him in return.

The earl had heard that jailers could be bribed to allow escapes to occur. He was hoping to flee to France until political circumstances were more favourable. But he needed a trusted person to bring him money. Maggie willingly made the journey, although she had never travelled further than the local market before.

One day a familiar sound drifted through the bars of the earl's cell. It was a song he recognised and he realised it was a signal. He called for the jailer and pleaded with him to go and find the lassie that was singing a Scots song from home. The earl would dearly like to hear another one. The jailer complied and a few minutes later Maggie was brought to the cell, complaining beautifully in her Borders' brogue. She had a basket of bannocks (oatcakes) on her arm and protested that she was on her way to market.

As soon as she was admitted to the cell, the earl pleaded with her for a song from home. Maggie pretended reluctance but her brown eyes were dancing as her sweet voice lilted through the jail. After a few airs the jailer came to take her away and Maggie pretended generosity to her fellow countryman and handed him two great fat bannocks. As Maggie left, the earl broke open the cakes to find enough gold coins to win him his freedom.

Some years later, when the earl returned to Lauderdale, he personally thanked Maggie Hardie. He had a fine silver-chain girdle made for this woman who was plucky and clever enough to save him.

If you visit the Museum of Scotland in Edinburgh, Maggie's girdle is on display for all to see.

✧ Aspen ✧

I received this tale from the traveller, Stanley Robertson. The aspen is a tree which is found across Scotland, and is known as 'the tree with the clattering tongues'. SB

A long time ago in the Borders of Scotland, a young farmer lived alone on an isolated farm. His animals and crops thrived, but often he longed for a wife with which to share his life. One day a young Gypsy girl set up camp in his woods. There was no one with her, but she seemed content to be alone. During the day she went round the countryside selling baskets and pegs which she made by her campfire in the evenings. She was very pretty and modest too, but after a month or so it became apparent that she was carrying a child.

Over the weeks the farmer fell in love with her, and as there was no sign of a partner, he plucked up his courage and one evening went to the woods and asked the lass to marry him.

'I dinna care that you're with child,' he told her. 'If you agree tae wed me, I'll bring the wee one up as my ain.'

And so it happened. The farmer and the Gypsy were married, and later in the year the wife was delivered of a fine baby girl.

She was quite, quite beautiful, except for one strange feature. Her hair was jet black, like that of her mother, but down the middle of her head ran a white zigzag streak, like a flash of lightning. The mother called her Aspen, after her favourite tree in the woods.

Within two years, the Gypsy bore the farmer a son, young Robert, and he adored his sister Aspen. As the two children grew, they were a great help and comfort to their parents, but when they had finished their chores, Aspen always went to her room to comb out her long hair before the mirror. She would brush out the day's tangles and hum a strange old tune in a very low voice, as her body swayed back and forth.

When Aspen was 15 years and a day, a stranger rode up the farm track. Robert was scything hay, and watched the tall man approach. He was wearing a black cape, a wide black slouched hat, gauntlets and boots; odd, for such a hot summer's day, the boy thought. The stranger was obviously wealthy; his saddle was fine Spanish leather, inlaid with silver, and the pouch at his side jingled heavily with coins.

It did not take long to discover the reason for his visit. The stranger told the farmer, 'The news of your daughter's great beauty has reached my lands, and I have come to see for myself, and perhaps ask her to marry me.'

'My dother will answer for hersel,' replied the farmer. 'I wad never force marriage on her.'

So saying, he pointed the stranger in the direction of Aspen's room, where she was seated combing out her beautiful black hair. The man quickly climbed the stairs, knocked and entered. She did not seem surprised or frightened to see him. The stranger bowed low, and explained his mission.

'I am not yet 16, sir,' she whispered demurely. 'Come back in a year's time, and I'll gie you my answer then.'

The stranger did not look best pleased, but with a grunt he turned away and left the room. He took his leave of Aspen's father, telling him to expect another visit in a year's time.

Robert, however, was deeply suspicious of the strange visitor, and without a word to anyone, decided to follow him. He kept his distance from the man so as not to be seen, and gradually night drew in. The stranger entered a wood, and Robert followed. The boy watched through the trees, as the stranger dismounted and bent down by a lochside; the water was gleaming in the moonlight between the pines. Robert saw the man kneel down, cup his hands to catch the water and then lap the water up to his mouth.

As the stranger drank, a horrid transformation began. His hands began to contort into the shape of long, black, hairy claws. His face changed too; it became long and lean and the teeth in the mouth were curved and rapacious. Then, the werewolf raised his head to the moon and howled. It was haunting and piercing with the weight of years of cruelty and sorrows within it.

Robert had seen enough to confirm his worst fears and quietly withdrew. He did not wish to alarm his little family, so he decided to keep the stranger's secret to himself. None of them could combat such a powerful creature; they did not have the skills in the black arts. His only hope was that the werewolf would not return.

The seasons passed and the farmer and his wife had almost forgotten about their daughter's strange suitor. But the werewolf had not forgotten. Exactly a year later the man returned; he was more determined than ever to have the Gypsy's daughter as his wife. This time, Aspen accepted his offer. Her parents were distraught to see her go, but the stranger assured them he had great wealth and power; Aspen would want for nothing as his wife. He scooped the lass up and set her up behind him on his horse, and set off for his castle and lands.

Robert had been working out in the fields and until he came home that night he knew nothing of the stranger's return and his sister's acceptance. When he learned how things had gone with his sister, he saddled the old farm horse and set off in pursuit, thinking perhaps to snatch Aspen away from the wicked creature. But after travelling for seven days, he began to despair of ever catching up with them.

On the seventh night, Robert came to a low glen at the foot of two high mountains. Rising up between the bens was a castle, black against the moon. Though it was night, he did not dare use the path, but led the horse through a wood. Through the trees he found a hut belonging to a hen wife. The wizened old woman was kind and invited Robert in for a bowl of nettle soup. He accepted thankfully, and after he had eaten he told her what had brought him to the area.

'Oh laddie,' the old crone muttered, 'this very nicht they are makin ready for the waddin tomorrow! I warn ye tae bide awa, the werewolf is a powerfu laird and an evil ane!'

Robert waited to hear no more, but journeyed on to try to save his sister. When he reached the castle, the guards asked who he was and why he had come and he lied saying he had come bringing wedding gifts for the bridegroom from a warlock far to the north, and that he had orders to give them immediately and personally into the master's hands. A guard directed him up a steep set of dark, winding stairs.

'The master is up there wi his bride tae be,' he told Robert. 'He left word nae tae be disturbed.'

At that moment there was a piercing shriek that turned Robert's blood to ice. Terrified that his sister had been murdered, he raced up to the room and forced open the door. There before him swayed a huge adder. She reached up to the roof and had a white zigzag stripe which stretched down her scales. The great snake looked down on Robert with her reptilian yellow eyes; her forked tongue flickered back and forth from her mouth, from which protruded fierce fangs. In the corner of the room a heap of black fur and blood lay huddled; it was the body of the werewolf, stone dead.

When the great adder saw Robert, a silver mist encircled her, then dispersed. Standing there was his beautiful sister, Aspen, looking as she always did.

'My real faither is the King o' the Adder tribe,' she told her half-brother. 'When he saw how kind the fairmer was tae my mither, he allowed them tae marry. But I hae my faither's powers. If I hadna agreed tae wed the werewolf, he micht hae killed ye aa. He little knew that I'd hae the killin o' him!'

The brother and sister returned home and never again did Aspen take the shape of an adder, though she always carried the lightning mark through her hair.

✧ The Ballad o' Tam Lin ✧

Carterhaugh is the name of a wood and a farm near Selkirk in the Borders where the Yarrow Water and the Ettrick Water meet. In this old Scots ballad which Robert Burns recycled, this location is the setting for an encounter between Tam Lin and the fairy queen. Translation of Scots is in brackets by each line. SB

O I forbid ye, maidens a, that wear gowd on your hair,
To come, and gae by Carterhaugh, for young Tam Lin is there.
There's nane that gaes by Carterhaugh, but they leave him a wad; (token)
Their rings, or green mantles, or else their maidenhead.

Janet has kilted her green kirtle, a little aboon her knee; (above)
And she has braided her yella hair a little aboon her bree; (brow)
And she's awa to Carterhaugh as fast as she can hie. (go)

When she came to Carterhaugh Tam Lin was at the well,
And there she fand his steed standing but away was himsel.
She had na pu'd a double rose, a rose but only twa,
Till up then started young Tam Lin, says,
'Lady, thou's pu' nae mair.' (pull no more)

'Why pu's thou the rose, Janet? And why breaks thou the wand? (stem)
Or why comes thou to Carterhaugh without when my command?'
'Carterhaugh it is my ain, my daddy gave it me;
I'll come and gae by Carterhaugh and ask nae leave at thee!'

Janet has kilted her green kirtle, a little aboon her knee;
And she has braided her yella hair a little aboon her bree;
And she's awa to Carterhaugh as fast as she can hie.

Four and twenty ladies fair were playing at the ba, (ball)
And out then cam fair Janet, aince the flower amang them a. (the first)
Four and twenty ladies fair were playing at the chess,
And out then came fair Janet, as green as onie grass.

Out then spak an auld grey knight, lay o'er the castle-wa, (wall)
And says, 'Alas, fair Janet for thee but we'll be blam'd a.' (we'll be blamed)
'Haud your tongue, ye auld-fac'd knight, some ill death may ye die!
Father my bairn on whom I will,
I'll father nane on thee!' (I'll not blame you)

Out then spak her father dear, and he spak meek and mild, (spoke)
'And ever alas, sweet Janet,' he says,
'I think thou gaes wi' child.' (with child)
'If that I gae wi' child, father, mysel maun bear the blame; (I am to blame)
There's ne'er a laird about your ha, shall get the bairn's name.'

'If my Love were an earthly knight, as he's an elfin grey
I was na gie my ain true-love for nae lord that ye hae. (not give)
The steed that my true love rides on, is lighter than the wind;
Wi' siller he is shod before, wi' burning gowd behind.' (silver … gold)

Janet has kilted her green kirtle, a little aboon her knee;
And she has braided her yella hair, a little aboon her bree;
And she's awa to Carterhaugh, as fast as she can hie.

When she came to Carterhaugh, Tam Lin was at the well,
And there she fand his steed standing, but away was himsel.
She had na pu'd a double rose, a rose but only twa,
Till up then started young Tam Lin, says, 'Lady thou pu's nae mair.
Why pu's thou the rose, Janet, amang the groves sae green,
And a' to kill the bonie babe, that we gat us between?'

'O tell me, tell me, Tam Lin,' says she,
'for's sake that died on tree, (God's sake)
If e'er ye were in holy chapel, or Christendom did see?'
'Roxburgh he was my Grandfather, took me with him to bide,
And aince it fell upon a day that wae did me betide.' (one day … woe)

'Aince it fell upon a day, a cauld day and a snell, (snowy)
When we were frae the hunting come, that frae my horse I fell.
The Queen o' Fairies she caught me, in yon green hill to dwell,
And pleasant is the fairyland but, an eerie tale to tell!

'Aye at the end of seven years, they pay a tiend to hell (fee of a human)
I am sae fair and fu' o' flesh I'm fear'd it be mysel.
But the night is Halloween, Lady, the morn is Hallowday;
Then win me, win me, an ye will, for weel I wat ye may.
Just at the mirk and midnight hour the fairie folk will ride,
And they that wad their true love win, at Miles Cross they maun bide.'

'But how shall I thee ken, Tam Lin, o' how my true love know
Amang sae mony unco knights the like I never saw?' (other)
'O first let pass the black, Lady,
and syne let pass the brown (horse colours)
But quickly run to the milk-white steed, pu ye his rider down!

'For I'll ride on a milk-white steed and aye nearest tae the town.
Because I was an earthly knight they gie me that renown. (permission)
My right hand will be glov'd, lady, my left hand will be bare;
Cockt up shall my bonnet be, and kaim'd down shall my hair;
And thae's the tokens I gie thee, nae doubt I will be there. (they are)

'They'll turn me in your arms, lady, into an asp and adder,
But hold me fast and fear me not, I am your bairn's father.
They'll turn me to a bear sae grim, and then a lion bold
But hold me fast and fear me not, as you shall love your child.

'Again they'll turn me in your arms to a red het gaud of airn (rod of iron)
But hold me fast and fear me not, I'll do to you nae harm.
And last they'll turn me, in your arms, into the burning lead
Then throw me into well-water, o' throw me in wi' speed!
And then I'll be your ain true love, I'll turn a naked knight:
Then cover me wi' your green mantle, and cover me out o' sight.'

Gloomy, gloomy was the night, and eerie was the way,
As fair Janet in her green mantle to Miles Cross she did gae.
About the middle o' the night she's heard the bridles ring;
This lady was as glad at that as any earthly thing.

First she let the black pass by, and syne she let the brown;
And quickly she ran to the milk-white steed and pu'd the rider down.
Sae weel she minded what he did say and young Tam Lin did win
Syne cover'd him wi' her green mantle as blythe's a bird in spring.

Out then spak the Queen o' Fairies, out o' a brush o' broom
'Them that hae gotten young Tam Lin hae gotten a stately groom.'
Out then spak the Queen o' Fairies, and an angry queen was she,
'Shame betide her ill-fard face, and an ill death may she die, (ugly)
For she's ta-en awa the boniest knight in a' my companie.
But had I kent, Tam Lin,' she says, 'what now this night I see,
I wad hae ta'en out thy twa grey een,
and put in twa een o' tree.' (eyes … wood)

GLASGOW CITY

✧ The Legends o' the Coat of Arms ✧

The coat of arms of the City of Glasgow incorporates symbols associated with Glasgow's patron saint, Mungo. They represent miracles supposedly performed by him and are listed in the traditional rhyme:

Here is the bird that never flew
Here is the tree that never grew
Here is the bell that never rang
Here is the fish that never swam GB

Here is the bird that never flew
According to legend, when he was a boy St Mungo was wrongfully blamed for the death of a robin which had been accidentally killed. When he took the dead bird in his hands, it was restored to life and flew back to its carer, St Mungo's master.

Here is the tree that never grew
Although the coat of arms depicts an oak tree, the miracle happened with a hazel branch. One night St Mungo was in charge of the monastery; part of his duty was to keep the fire going. But he had fallen asleep and some of his enemies put out the fire. When he awoke to find the fire cold, he went out, cut some hazel branches

placed them in the brazier and prayed over them. Immediately they burst into flames.

Here is the bell that never rang
The priest was given a bell, some say by the Pope, which remained an important symbol when St Mungo died, and it was cherished for centuries by the people of Glasgow until its disappearance in 1574. A replica was made in 1641, which can still be seen in The People's Palace Museum.

Here is the fish that never swam
During the time that St Mungo was a priest in Glasgu, which means 'beloved green place', the king who ruled there had a beautiful wife. As a token of his love the king gave her a ring, which the queen gave to a knight with whom she was affectionate. Unfortunately, while out hunting with this knight, the king saw a ring on his servant's finger which looked familiar. While the knight slept, the king threw the ring into the river Clyde and on returning home he demanded that his wife show him her ring. The queen sought out the knight, who could not return it and in panic she went and confessed her problems to the priest. St Mungo asked one of his priests to go fishing and bring back the first fish that he caught. When it was cut open the ring was within.

St Mungo is also said to have preached a sermon containing the words 'Lord, let Glasgow flourish.' This was shortened to 'Let Glasgow Flourish' and became the city's motto.

✧ The Glasgow Vampire ✧

I think my grandmother's scariest tale originated in Glasgow. She listened avidly to the news on the wireless, and would relay more dramatic extracts from news items to me. I was 7 when she told me the story of the Glasgow vampire. The myth took root in the centre of the Glasgow Southern Necropolis in the Gorbals district in 1954; people believed that there was a vampire abroad in the cemetery, with iron teeth.

The rumour spread that the monster had killed two children. Things reached such a pitch adults blamed the influence of American horror comics. The Children and Young Persons (Harmful Productions) Act was introduced in 1955, which banned the sale of comics and magazines that showed 'incidents of a repulsive or horrible nature' to minors.

My own comics were quite innocent affairs, the Beano, *the* Dandy *and 'Oor Willie' in the* Sunday Post, *lots of violent children but not a vampire in sight! SB*

The tale began when Constable Alex Deeprose was called out to the graveyard on the evening of 23 September 1954. He was astounded by what confronted him. Hundreds of children armed with knives and sharpened sticks were walking through the cemetery. They were aged between 4 and 14 and were hunting a 7-foot-high vampire who had already, they claimed, eaten two children with his iron teeth. A local headmaster told them the story was ridiculous, but the huge army of children returned over the next two nights until the frenzy abated.

Ronnie Sanderson was 8 at the time, and described how the myth began:

> It all started in the playground; someone said there was a vampire in the graveyard and everyone was going to head out there after school. At three o'clock the school emptied and everyone made a beeline for it. We sat there for ages on the wall waiting and waiting. I wouldn't go in because it was a bit scary for me. I think somebody saw a man wandering about and people began to shout, '*There's a Vampire!*' I just remember scampering home to my mother and she said, 'What's the matter with you?'

I said, 'I've seen a vampire!'

I got a clout round the ear for my trouble. I didn't really know what a vampire was.

✧ Kingston Bridge ✧

As might be expected from such determined and quirky citizens, Glasgow's urban myths do not disappoint. The Kingston Bridge crosses the river Clyde and is one of the busiest in Europe. Work began on the bridge in 1966 and it was officially declared open by Queen Elizabeth, the Queen Mother, in 1970.

I heard the following tale from a Glasgow tour guide on an open-topped bus on an unusually sunny day two years ago. SB

There was a Glasgow gang in the 1960s, which violently robbed the British Linen Bank in Williamwood. Their get-away driver was a man called Archibald McGeachie. Following the robbery McGeachie disappeared; he had gone to collect his car from a garage but never arrived and was never seen again. He had £60 in cash and a bankbook with him but nothing was ever withdrawn from his account again. His father was convinced that his son had been murdered. It is widely believed that McGeachie was buried in cement inside the pillars of the Kingston Bridge, killed for refusing to take part in another robbery. Police later found bloodstained clothes and a spade near to the bridge. The handle of the spade was splattered with blood and the actual blade was covered with cement and earth.

This bridge is rumoured to be a concrete grave for several infamous gangsters who vanished in unexplained circumstances in the late 1960s. It is reputed that the Mafia-style Glasgow godfather of crime, Arthur Thomson, ordered them killed and buried within the concrete piers of the bridge while it was being built.

X-rays were taken of the pillars and revealed that there are indeed skeletons trapped within the concrete of Kingston Bridge. But dismantling the bridge would be very disruptive and costly so it was decided to leave the remains of the victims in their unusual grave.

✧ The Rocking Chair ✧

This is an urbanised, contemporary version of an old Scottish legend told to me by the late Stanley Robertson. SB

White Mary and Black Mary lived with their mother Mrs Snapper in a high-rise flat in Glasgow. White Mary was beautiful; she had silky blond hair, while Black Mary, her stepsister, had knotty, dark hair. Mrs Snapper was White Mary's stepmother; she was a cruel, hard-hearted woman. When White Mary was 5, her father died and since then, she was made to clean the house for Black Mary and Mrs Snapper, working her fingers to the bone every day.

Until she was 16, White Mary was treated abominably. The three of them lived on the nineteenth floor of the high rise, and the lift broke down nearly every day. When this happened poor White Mary had to toil up and down nineteen flights of stairs, lugging the shopping. After that, she had to cook, clean and do everything around the flat.

On the morning of her sixteenth birthday, White Mary looked forlornly out of the window at the tiny figure of the postman delivering parcels far below. Would he bring her a card? No card came. The day went on as usual until it turned dark. After White Mary had washed up the supper dishes, Mrs Snapper made an announcement.

'I've kept ye for 16 years. I'll nae get a penny aff the social for ye noo. Yer nae my responsibility onymair. Get oot!'

White Mary was horrified, 'But whaur'll I go? I've nae money!'

'Nae my concern,' replied Mrs Snapper, shoving the poor girl out of the door.

As usual, the lift was broken. Poor White Mary trudged down all the flights of stairs, into the dark, dangerous streets amongst drunks and gangs and junkies, for they lived in the poorest part of the city. Terrified, she walked till she came to some allotments. There was a shed on each allotment, and she found one in which she could shelter; it looked slightly better than the rest and had a rocking chair outside on the path. She opened the gate and walked up the overgrown path.

She was just about to open the door, when to her astonishment the rocking chair spoke, 'Yer wantin intae this sheddie, aren't ye?'

'I am,' she replied nervously.

'I'm feelin affa hot,' continued the chair. 'If ye sprinkle some fine cool watter ontae ma seat, I'll tell ye somethin important.'

Being a kind-natured girl, White Mary took a watering can and walked to the foot of the allotments where there was a tinkling stream. Returning, she sprinkled the rocking chair.

It sighed, contentedly. 'Ah,' it said, 'that's grand!'

The rocking chair told her that the shed was like Dr Who's police box. Inside, it was huge and luxurious. It warned White Mary that as soon as she entered the shed, the Devil would appear before her, for he owned the place. The chair advised her to take a pail inside with her, for when the Devil saw White Mary, he would ask her to dance with him. She was to agree to this if he filled her pail with gold. The chair warned White Mary to find excuses not to dance with the Devil until the cock crowed at dawn. After that he would lose his power, and would have to go back to Hell. But if she danced with him, she would be his forever.

Things went exactly as the rocking chair had said. The instant she stepped into the shed, White Mary was astonished to find it looked like a sumptuous ballroom, with chandeliers, thick carpets and heavy velvet curtains. She was just recovering from the shock, when a cloud of sulphur and brimstone suddenly erupted before her eyes, and the Devil appeared, wearing a black silk cape. His eyes were like two live coals; he bowed very low, and asked her to dance with him. White Mary agreed, on condition that he filled her pail with gold to the very brim. Suddenly, she heard the tinkle of coin, and from nowhere, gold fell thick and fast into the pail.

The Devil stepped forward to dance with her, but White Mary pointed to her hair.

'I couldna possibly dance wi you like this,' she said. 'My hair is all tousled and dirty. I need it shampooed an caimbed. I need extensions and highlights pit in.'

The Devil ground his teeth, but he sent to Hell to fetch his best hairdresser to fulfil her request. Again the Devil stepped forward to dance with her, but White Mary pointed to her dress.

'I couldna possibly dance wi you like this,' she said. 'Look at these rags I'm wearin. I need a frock frae Paris, a real ball goun, wi a low back an spangles.'

The Devil growled and hissed and stamped his cloven hooves, but he sent to Hell to fetch his best French dressmakers to fulfil her request. Once more the Devil stepped forward to dance with her, but White Mary pointed to her feet, 'I couldna possibly dance wi you like this, look at the state of my feet. I need a foot massage an a chiropodist, an wee fishies tae nibble aff the hard skin. An I need stiletto shoes, cherry red.'

The Devil flicked his tail and whirled his eyeballs round in their sockets, but he sent to Hell to fetch his best chiropodists and shoemakers to fulfil her request.

Eagerly the Devil stepped forward to dance with her, but White Mary said, 'I couldna possibly dance wi you like this,' pointing to her face. 'Look at my face; I need a full facial, eyebrows tweezed, lipstick an mascara.'

By now the Devil was absolutely furious, but he sent to Hell to fetch his best Hollywood makeup consultants to fulfil her request. Warily, the Devil stepped forward to dance with her, but White Mary pointed to her armpits.

'I couldna possibly dance wi you like this,' she said. 'Smell my oxters. I only ever got a Glasgow shower (a slosh of deodorant) at my step-mother's flat. I need a wash and perfume and deodorant and a razor, for I am Scottish, ye ken, nae European. We shave oor oxters here.'

The Devil clenched his fists and hissed even louder, but he sent to Hell to fetch his best Italian perfumier to fulfil her request.

Once more the Devil stepped forward to dance with her, but White Mary pointed to her neck and said, 'I couldna possibly dance wi you like this, look at my neck. It's bare. I need jewels; earrings, a necklace, a bracelet, rings … an a wee tattoo o' a dove.'

Sensing that time was running out, the Devil ground his teeth, but he sent to Hell to fetch his best jewellers and tattooists to fulfil her request.

By now, poor White Mary was desperate; she had run out of excuses. Just as the Devil was about to whirl her away, the cock began to crow. The Devil with a shriek of rage was forced back to the depths of Hell. White Mary was left with a pail full of gold and all the gifts that the Devil had showered on her. She stepped from the shed into the bright sunshine, thanked the rocking chair, gave it another spray of cold water and flagged down a taxi.

When she reached her stepmother's block of flats, she found the lift was working. Up she went to the nineteenth floor and rang her stepmother's doorbell. Mrs Snapper opened the door, thinking White Mary was the council lady who had come to serve an eviction notice for rent arrears. White Mary told her stepmother all about the shed, and left sixteen gold coins with Mrs Snapper from her pail, one coin for every year she had been given a roof over her head. Then she turned and left.

Mrs Snapper's mind was in a whirl. She went through and prodded Black Mary who was lying on the sofa.

'Get up tae the allotments an bring a pail o' gold back for us!'

As it was turning dark, Black Mary took a taxi up to the

allotments and told the taxi driver to wait for her. The rocking chair looked at Black Mary and did not like what it saw.

'I'm feelin affa hot,' said the chair. 'If ye sprinkle some fine cool watter ontae ma seat, I'll tell ye somethin important.'

Being a bad-tempered, selfish girl, Black Mary walked to the nearest stinking puddle, scooped up a rusty can full of water and flung it over the rocking chair. The chair shuddered in disgust. It told her about the Devil, and how he would ask her to dance, and it told her to request the pail to be filled with gold, but it did not say any more.

Black Mary marched into the shed. Immediately, the Devil appeared, bowed low, and asked her to dance with Him.

'Fill this pail wi gold first!' cried the rude girl.

The pail mysteriously filled with gold. Then the Devil took Black Mary in his hairy arms, and whirled her round the floor until her feet bled. When the cock crowed Black Mary bent down to pick up her pail of gold. But before her eyes, the coins changed from gold into dry dead leaves. Instantly, Black Mary began to change. From the top of her head down, she disintegrated, until there was only a little pile of dust on the shed floor. From nowhere, a wind rose up and blew the dust into the nettle patch outside. Laughing loudly, the Devil flew back to Hell. And for all I know the taxi driver is still waiting outside for his fare.

✧ Overtoun Dogs ✧
– an urban legend fae West Dunbartonshire

Overtoun House in West Dunbartonshire was built in the 1860s. There is a bridge on the way leading to the house, built from locally quarried granite. It spans the rocky Overtoun Burn, 50 feet below. It has been reported that fifty or more dogs have leapt off the bridge to their death since the 1950s. Why should apparently normal dogs leap to their death off this bridge? SB

The Cooper family were the owners of a border collie named Ben and were out walking their dog one bright sunny morning. But as they crossed the Overtoun Bridge, the collie suddenly leapt the stone parapet and fell to his death 50 feet below.

Another dog owner had a similar experience at almost exactly the same spot. His golden retriever had leapt over and fallen, but landed on a bank. Although she had no serious physical injury, the shock caused all her hair to fall out.

Many strange theories have been put forward about the reason for the animal deaths, including ghosts or perhaps dogs sensitised to depression. Overtoun is also known as a 'thin place' where the spiritual realm is very close.

Concern about the ongoing deaths caused one man to return to the scene of his dog's 'suicide' jump many years later. His dog had lived through the experience and although she was now 19, he walked her over the bridge to see how she would react. At exactly the same spot where she had previously jumped, the dog stopped and was obviously agitated but was too old now to jump up. The owner knew she could not see above the parapet, as it was too high, she could not hear because she was deaf, so he deduced the dog's reaction could only be connected with smell.

Looking back at common factors the dogs only jumped on sunny, dry days and only on the right-hand side of the bridge and all the dogs had been of certain breeds that have long snouts.

A scientist checked the undergrowth and discovered signs of mice and mink, which were released from captivity in the 1950s and have multiplied since. The 'suicides' have only occurred since that time. The RSPCA conducted tests on ten dogs to see how they would react to the scents of mice and mink in a field. Eight out of ten ran straight to the mink scent.

The conclusion is that in all probability the dogs, sadly, reacted to mink scent below the bridge and the overriding impulse was to jump.

✧ The Little Buddy Hoax ✧ – an urban legend fae Paisley

Over coffee, a friend of mine was chatting about effective hoaxes that have managed to dupe people and a man at the next table overheard us. He was American and told us about an article his niece had read concerning The Little Buddy Hoax in Paisley back in March 1987; it was titled 'Myth Produces Mountain Of Mail For "Dying Boy"'. SB

A Scottish boy had been dying of cancer and his one wish was to see his name in print in the *Guinness Book of Records* for collecting the largest number of postcards in the world. Through the media, the message had gone worldwide and many people responded, sending postcards to a postbox in Paisley. It was estimated that 'Little Buddy' received more than four million postcards but towards the end of 1983 the postal workers stopped counting. It was discovered that the boy did not exist; no one had ever come to collect the postcards and the post office was left with mountains of unclaimed mail.

Apparently, some years later, the hoax was restarted, much to the chagrin of the postal workers!

ARGYLL AND THE INNER ISLES

✧ A Dragonish Tale ✧

A long time ago there was a magnificent hill fort called Dunardy in Argyll, which had been the stronghold of the Mactavish clan over many generations. SB

One morning the chief's eldest son went out to the great moss to hunt. He succeeded in killing a stag, and was gutting the beast when a thick white mist descended. The hunter hauled his kill up onto his pony and, leading her forward, he strode in the direction he thought was home. But by evening he was totally disorientated and was growing increasingly worried when he came upon a cairn with a doorway in it; light was pouring out from within. The man unloaded his pony and tied her to a tree and entered the cairn.

To his astonishment he found a sleeping dragon, curled up on top of a pile of bones and gold. He tried to retreat carefully but unluckily he dislodged a stone and wakened the dragon. Thinking quickly he slammed the door shut and blocked it with the body of the stag. This was no deterrent to a dragon; it was not held off for long, it heaved aside the door and rapidly gave chase. Dragons are nocturnal, and although their eyesight is poor, they have a very strong sense of smell. Thinking swiftly Mactavish managed to catch hold of another deer. He flung his plaid over its antlers and let it flee in the direction of the pursuing dragon.

He blew his horn to alert his kinsmen in the hill fort, and then plunged into a forest to try and draw the dragon away from his people. The creature smelt him in the darkness, and pursued him through the trees. It would have overcome him, but suddenly a huge wild boar rushed out of the thickets behind. Its breath was blue in the misty night air and its eyes gleamed gold. Its bristles were strong as spears. The dragon turned to face its huge adversary and both charged at the other. The impact was heard for miles and the creatures crashed together with such force that both were killed immediately.

The hunter's father, chief of the clan, on hearing the story, cut off the boar's head and raised it in a place of honour. Today the boar's head is still used as the clan's symbol.

The rocks that were cloven in two where the beasts died in combat is known as the Beastie Stone, in Glenn-na-Beistie, the Glen of the Beast by the Dunardry locks on the Crinan Canal.

✧ The Fairy's Substitute ✧

A changeling is said to be a child left by the elf folk in place of a real baby. In the Orkney and Shetland islands it was thought that trolls coveted human children. It was widely believed across Scotland that a baby born with a caul across its face is a changeling, of supernatural origin. People used many ways to test if a child was a changeling or not.

Fairy folk preferred newly born children and their mothers. Until the mothers were 'sained' and churched and the newborn child had been baptised, they were in grave danger, as every seven years the fairies had to pay a 'teind to hell' which they attempted to pay with a human child.

✧ A Vexing Child ✧ – a legend fae Kintallen

This story comes from a small village called Kintallen, which is on the shores of Loch Sween, near Lochgilphead on the west coast of Scotland. SB

In Kintallen, a woman had a son who ate like a horse and wailed non-stop. While others were off harvesting, she could not join them, because of the horrible screaming and behaviour of the boy. At that time there was a tailor lodging in the house. He was suspicious of the child, and offered to look after him while the mother joined the other workers in the field. She had hardly left the room before the creature began wailing and screeching again.

'Stop that now,' said the tailor, 'or I'll throw you onto the fire.'

This silenced the boy for a time but soon he set off yowling again.

'Any more noise from you and I'll stab you to death!'

This worked for a little while, but when the howling started up again, the tailor went to the cradle and flung a set of bagpipes into the crib.

'Make a tune on that,' the tailor growled, 'or I'll stab you.'

Frightened, the changeling sat up in its bed and played the sweetest bagpipe music ever heard. When the workers returned from the fields the tailor took the mother aside and told her to take the baby to Ardsheil bay and throw it into the loch. The woman did as she was bid and when the creature touched the water it changed into a grey-haired wizened old man and swam off. On returning home the woman found her own child lying there, restored to her.

✧ The Fairies' Craftsman ✧ – a legend fae Islay

In some situations, what may at first appear a tragedy can be turned for good. This legend from Islay is a changeling tale but with an unusual ending. GB

On the island of Islay in a place called Crosprig, there lived a blacksmith called MacEachern, with his wife and son. When their son was 14, he began to sicken, and there was no relief. His skin began to yellow and grow wrinkled and wizened. The healthy, lively boy that his parents knew was gone, and instead, a listless invalid lay on the cot, growing weaker and weaker with each passing day.

The blacksmith and his wife were very worried, and so the father decided to go and visit the wise man of the village. The blacksmith explained to the man what was wrong with his son.

'I believe the fairies have been,' said the man. 'Now go home, blacksmith, and do exactly as I say.'

The blacksmith returned home and followed the wise man's instructions carefully. In sight of the cot and the boy, he took a number of eggshells and placed them in a circle in front of the fireplace. Then, taking a jug, he carefully filled each one with water. A squawk came from the bed. Startled, the blacksmith turned round to see a yellow, wrinkled mannequin sit up in the cot, leering, 'Never in my 800 years have I seen anything so queer as what you have just done!'

Raucously, the creature began to laugh. Absolutely convinced that this was indeed a fairy changeling, the blacksmith returned to the wise man and told him what had happened.

'Now ma man, you must throw that creature on the fire!' The blacksmith looked horrified, but the wise man hastily assured him, 'Dinna worry, for if that *is* your son, he will cry out afore you have the chance to throw him in, but if it is indeed a changeling, it will fly up the chimney and never return!'

The blacksmith returned home and built up the fire. Without giving himself time to hesitate, he quickly took the creature up in his arms and threw it on the fire. With a shriek, it flew up the chimney, and never darkened the blacksmith's door again. But what of the couple's own son? Where had he gone? The wise man advised the blacksmith that if he wanted his son back, he must go to the fairy hill at Borraichill to reclaim his child, but this could only happen on the night of Hallow's Eve.

Impatiently, the blacksmith had to wait for some weeks before the night came, but it gave him time to plan. At midnight on Hallow's Eve he made his way to the fairy knoll, which was emanating light and music from an opening in the hill. He had come carefully prepared. In one hand, he held a bible to protect him from the evil of the fairies. In his belt he had his sharp metal dirk, and as he passed over the threshold into the fairy kingdom, he thrust the dagger into the earth to prevent the door closing upon him and trapping him there forever. On his shoulder he carried a sleeping cockerel.

Before him, fairies were dancing and carousing, the floor was a whirl of movement and laughter, and there was food and drink flowing, but the blacksmith was not distracted. His eyes searched and searched for a sight of a familiar figure. Suddenly the blacksmith saw his son standing at the back of the hall, and he cried out his name. Immediately, the fairies all turned on the stranger and demanded to know his business.

'I have come to reclaim my son that you stole from me! You must give him back!' demanded the father.

The fairies looked to him and at each other in surprise, then all burst out laughing, and mocked the blacksmith for thinking he could remove his son from their grasp. But as the noise of their cruel laughter filled the fairy hall, the cockerel stirred, opened its eyes, stood upright, stretched its neck and let out a piercing crow. At once, the lights went out, the music ceased and all the fairies vanished, for they could not remain after the cockerel had crowed.

The hall entrance began to close. Grabbing his son's hand, the blacksmith ran hell for leather out of the opening. Never had the night air smelt so sweet; he had his son back! With great joy, the father clasped his son to his breast, and led the bewildered lad home.

But over the next months, it was as if the boy had almost no memory of his own home and family. His parents treated him gently and lovingly, but he hardly spoke or engaged with them in any way.

One day, the blacksmith was out at his forge. He was working on his anvil in the intense heat, hammering and shaping metal into a sword. He was very aware that his son was standing near, watching intently. Suddenly his son spoke. 'Father, that is not the way to fashion a good sword. Let me show you; I know a better way.'

Surprised but pleased, the blacksmith looked at the lad. The boy's eyes were intense and focused; the vacant stare was gone. The father smiled, and handed over his gloves and tools, then watched in amazement as slowly and expertly, the boy began to fashion the most beautiful sword he had ever seen. When it was complete, the blacksmith shook his head in wonder as he examined the intricate designs his son had worked upon the metal. Never had he seen anything so perfect. 'This sword is only fit for a king, my lad!'

With his son's agreement, they travelled to the court of the Lord of the Isles and presented the sword to him, where it was received with great appreciation.

From that day forward, the blacksmith was never short of business. His son had learnt his trade well from the fairies. The family were appointed swordsmiths to the Lords of the Isles, and continued to craft well-tempered weapons of exceptional quality for a long time to come.

Still to this day, the sword of Islay is remembered as the Islay Hilt or in Gaelic, the Claidheamh Ceann Ile.

✧ A Hollow Victory ✧
– a legend fae Taynuilt, Oban

Near Oban is a place called Taynuilt, which thrived in the late eighteenth and early nineteenth centuries as a result of pig iron manufacture, which was a very successful export. In the Bonawe Ironworks, cannonballs were made; vital munitions in the ongoing Napoleonic Wars. Cannonballs were a product of which the workers were very proud.

There were 600 local Gaelic speakers employed in this business, most of whom were coalers. They harvested wood, which they burnt to make charcoal, used to fuel the ironworks. This was a summer job only.

The surrounding Argyll forests were ideal for supplying the quantity of charcoal needed to fire the ironworks' furnace. All through the woods during the summer months there would be charcoal burners smoking; the men would carefully monitor the slow burning of the wood to ensure quality charcoal was produced.

But what would the men do during the winter? For they still had mouths to feed. One popular and productive venture was the illicit creation of whisky. Crops would be sown and harvested with the intention of making this bracing alcohol. But where could the men safely distil their product, away from the prying eyes of the excisemen, known as gaugers? The process required cold, fast running water, of which there was plenty in the forests of Argyll!

The success of this venture depended largely on a good lookout system. Even so, gaugers were fly, and could often smell out a still. Although many stories are told of these entrepreneurs escaping the arm of the law, on this particular day, the gaugers appeared to be triumphant! GB

With great difficulty, the government men had made their way up by a waterfall known in Gaelic as Eas nan Caorach Dubha, or the Falls of the Black Sheep. The gaugers were delighted to find a number of stills nestled amongst the rocks, but better yet, there, sitting on a flat stone, was a full barrel of whisky. The distillers had not had time to remove it before the excisemen had puffed up the glen.

Wretchedly, the whisky men watched from their hiding places as the gaugers dismantled their gear and, licking their lips in anticipation, discussed how best to get the barrel down the glen without damaging it.

Eventually, with the help of ropes, the men carefully descended the steep path with their heavy, precious load, and made their way back through the forest to where they had left the horse and cart. Cheerily, they hoisted the barrel and equipment up onto the cart and, pleased with their day's work, they travelled to the White Inn in Kilchrennen, where they planned to stay for the night.

Once there, they told the innkeeper they would all bunk down in one room with the keg of whisky. They were anticipating a good dram, but though it was tempting, they had to return the whisky barrel completely full or else there would be questions asked. Reluctantly, the innkeeper gave the gaugers his room upstairs so they could all bunk down together, with the barrel carefully placed in the middle of the room.

After a fine supper, the men were replete and yawning; all the fresh air and exertion of their day's work had exhausted them and they were ready for a good night's sleep.

As soon as the innkeeper heard the sound of snoring, a signal was given, and quietly, a group of men entered the inn with a few contraptions in tow. Using stepladders, a hole was carefully bored into the ceiling directly beneath the barrel of whisky that was standing on the floor above. Immediately, whisky began to stream down and was caught in buckets, bowls and other containers. The smell of the spirit filled the room. After some time, the last drops were drained and the hole in the ceiling was carefully disguised. Bright eyed and grinning the conspirators left, well pleased with their evening's work.

In the morning, the gaugers awoke, stretched and ate a leisurely breakfast, still feeling cocksure after their previous day's success. What was their horror when braced to carry the heavy barrel downstairs, it slipped to the floor and the lid gently bounced off! Only the angel's share of the whisky was left.

The gaugers left the inn, shamefaced and furious, tricked yet again, and not one dram to show for it.

Meanwhile, the men, fuelled by a nip of whisky, had plans underway for their new stills; it would not be long before the *uisge-beatha* would be flowing once more!

✧ A Boon or Herald of Doom? ✧ – a legend fae the Isle of Skye

When visiting Dunvegan Castle on the Isle of Skye, you will see the fairy flag on display. It is an ancient relic, and if examined, faded red elf-spots can be seen upon the silk fabric that once had a brilliant yellow hue. Some say it was brought back from the Crusades, but although the material originated in the Middle East, it has been dated to between the fourth and seventh centuries, well before that time. Others firmly believe the flag was a gift bestowed to the Macleod clan by the fairy folk. GB

Many years ago, there was a clan chief who was loved by a fairy woman. They were happy for a time, and the woman gave birth to a fine young son. Sadly, the couple parted soon after the child was born. Perhaps the fairy tired of the mundane mortal life and longed once more for her homeland. Or was Macleod unfaithful to his love, and slighted, the broken-hearted fairy returned to her own kind?

Whatever the reason, Macleod was left with his newborn son, and as was the tradition, a feast was held in honour of the birth. During the happy celebrations, a young maid was watching over the bairn upstairs. He was sound asleep and in the silence of the tower room the maid became restless, and longed to join the lively throng below. She decided she could leave the child for a short time and made her way down the spiral staircase to the great hall.

While she was away, the bairn woke with a start, and began to cry. When comfort was not provided, his cries became more pitiful. Though his mother was now far from the castle, she could hear the wails of her child, and swiftly she came and comforted him.

She wrapped him in a silken covering, which seemed to soothe the bairn, and he settled back to sleep.

When the young maid returned to the chamber, she was gripped with fear when she saw the bairn was now covered in a bright yellow mantle with red elf-spots. Who or what had entered the chamber while she had been gone? The maid had been ordered to go and fetch the chief's son to show the guests the newborn heir. Hesitantly, she picked up the bairn, still wrapped in the mantle, and took him downstairs. When the maid entered the hall with the bairn, the sound of fairy music filled the great hall, and a prophecy rang out concerning the magical silken cloth. This flag might be raised to save Clan Macleod from mortal danger, three times only, but, the voice warned, it should never be lifted except in the direst of circumstances; if the gift were misused, there would be terrible consequences.

On hearing the prophecy, the chief immediately took precautions to protect the fairy gift from misuse. He ordered the flag to be taken and placed in a secured chest, which, from then on, could only be opened by the clan chief. It remained under lock and key for years, as one chief after another died and others took their place.

During a time of unrest, a fierce battle broke out between the Macdonalds and the Macleods. After many gruelling hours of hard fighting, the Macleod chief knew his men were close to defeat. He called for the ancient chest to be brought forth. He unlocked it, and withdrew the delicate relic. The chief hoisted the flag aloft and waved it before his enemies. Immediately, the tide of battle began to turn; it seemed that the Macleods had risen with new valour and strength, and the Macdonalds were routed.

Many years later, another catastrophe smote the Macleod clan. Plague almost wiped out the cattle on the island, and once more, the flag was waved. At once, the pestilence ceased and the diseased cattle recovered.

However, the third time the flag was raised, it was under very different circumstances. It had been locked away, untouched for hundreds of years, but in 1799, one sceptical man decided to prove this piece of cloth had no magical properties. He would show that the stories told of the flag were all just superstition.

While the chief was journeying away from Skye, this man carried out his plan. He had access to the room in which the relic was contained. The man hired a blacksmith, a foreigner with no knowledge or superstitious belief in the fairy flag. The blacksmith removed the iron clasps from the chest, and the sceptic opened it up, and took out the old, fragile fabric. Mockingly he waved the faded flag for the third time.

Within twelve months, this careless action invoked the three-fold curse of which the fairies had warned many centuries before.

The prophecy had declared that the heir to Clan Macleod would die prematurely, and within months, the successor was blown up in a tragic sea disaster while aboard the HMS *Charlotte*.

Secondly, it had been said a rocky outcrop on the coast, known as the Three Maidens, would be sold to a Campbell, and so it was.

That same year, there happened to be a lieutenant staying at the castle who kept a tame fox. It gave birth to cubs in one of the turret chambers, and this had been the third prediction.

When all three signs were fulfilled, it ushered in the final calamity, the foretold demise of Clan Macleod. It became impoverished, and many estates had to be sold.

In 1814, Sir Walter Scott visited Dunvegan and was shown the various relics on display. This was his description of the fairy flag's magical properties: 'Produced in battle, it multiplied the numbers of the Macleods; spread on the nuptial bed, it ensured fertility; and lastly, it brought herring into the loch.'

Still today, many hold fast to the aura that surrounds this ancient piece of silk, and wonder, what if it was raised again? What could happen?

OUTER HEBRIDES

✧ Finders but Not Keepers ✧ – a legend fae South Uist

From 1370 until 1839 the Clanranald ruled South Uist, which was known as a centre for religious instruction; by the seventeenth century it boasted two churches and three chapels. During the sixteenth century, the Clanranald chief was Iain Muideartaich; he funded the building of a chapel built at Howmore, an ancient religious site, where he was later buried. The place of worship was named Caibeal Chlann 'ic Ailean, or Clanranald's Chapel.

As the centuries passed the building fell into disrepair but a stone panel that had been embedded in one of the chapel's walls remained in good condition when the wall collapsed. It was made from sandstone quarried from Carsaig on the Isle of Mull. It was shaped like a square with a triangular top and carved with the arms of Clanranald.

The panel was left on the ground propped up against the graveyard wall, exposed to all weathers. GB

One July day in 1990, a small car stopped on the road near the ruins and two men hopped out. They both had a wander around the church and chapel remains and one noticed a heavy panel leaning, neglected, against a drystane dyke. There was some discussion between the friends and one of the men returned to the car. He drove it over the grass until it was close to the ruined chapel.

The two men heaved the stone up with great difficulty and carefully placed it in the car boot. Without a backward glance, the men hopped into their car and drove away.

Three months later a local man was out for a stroll; he had not walked by the church remains in a while. As he passed the Clanranald Chapel he stopped and scratched his head. He looked over the dyke and around the other side of the chapel. Puzzled, he frowned and headed back to his house.

The police were notified about the missing panel, but nothing was done, as there was no one who could actually claim ownership of the stone. Apparently there was no 'defacement' or 'desecration' to the walls of the chapel, nor the actual gravestones, which were the responsibility of the Department of the Environment. The panel was not regarded under either category. Despite appeals and media coverage, it had no effect; the stone had vanished and was gone without trace.

In November 1995, the British Museum had a strange phone call from Euston, London. A man claimed to have found what appeared to be an ancient reliquary stone in an apartment in the city, along with photographs of its 'removal'.

Gradually the story began to emerge; a couple who lived in Canada had come over to clear their son's flat. It was then they had found the stone and the photographs. From the description the stone was recognised and after undergoing a clean-up, it was returned to the South Uist Historical Society, who deemed it prudent to display it in the local museum of Kildonan rather than risk losing it to other potential trophy hunters.

It came to light that the young man who was the thief had died suddenly in his sleep at the age of 33. Locals from South Uist seemed to recall that in past times people believed a curse would fall on anyone who pillaged the ancient site at Howmore; they would die at a young age.

✧ The Mystery of Flannan Isle and the Cormorants ✧ – a legend fae near Lewis

The Flannan Isles lie eighteen miles off the west coast of Lewis. The three keepers at that time were James Ducat, Thomas Marshall and Donald McArthur. On 15 December 1900, the keepers of the lighthouse on Flannan Isle entered their last notes of barometer and thermometer readings in the log book. A steamer passed the lighthouse at midnight and noted that no light was visible, but unfortunately this was not reported. SB

On the afternoon of Boxing Day the *Hesperus* arrived on a routine visit. Captain Harvey, who was in command of the ship, fired a rocket to alert the lighthouse staff but there was no response. Joseph Moore, the relief keeper, disembarked to investigate but found the island and lighthouse deserted. Bewildered, he found everything as normal. The lamp was ready to be lit, suggesting that the three keepers had disappeared on the afternoon of 15 December. Evidence pointed to extremely bad weather in the area when the men went missing; Moore found the entrance gate and outside gates closed. The fire was unlit, the clock had stopped and the men's beds were empty. The kitchen pots and pans had been cleaned and all was tidy. How the men had met their end was a complete mystery.

Locally, it was known that cormorants were often spotted around those parts, and in the Western Isles, folk still believed that men often took the shape of sea creatures, such as seals, changing shape and adopting the life of their chosen creature.

Twelve years after the mysterious disappearance, Wilfred Wilson Gibson wrote a poem which seemed to accept this legend as a possible solution.

Extracts from 'Flannan Isle' by Wilfred Wilson Gibson

And, as into the tiny creek
We stole beneath the hanging crag,
We saw three queer, black, ugly birds
Too big, by far, in my belief,
For guillemot or shag
Like seamen sitting bold upright
Upon a half-tide reef:
But, as we near'd, they plunged from sight,
Without a sound, or spurt of white.

And still too mazed to speak,
We landed; and made fast the boat;
And climb'd the track in single file,
Each wishing he was safe afloat,
On any sea, however far,
So it be far from Flannan Isle:
And still we seem'd to climb, and climb,
As though we'd lost all count of time,
And so must climb for evermore.
Yet, all too soon, we reached the door
The black, sun-blister'd lighthouse door,
That gaped for us ajar [...]

We hunted high, we hunted low,
And soon ransack'd the empty house;
Then o'er the island, to and fro,
We ranged, to listen and to look
In every cranny, cleft or nook
That might have hid a bird or mouse:
But, though we searched from shore to shore,
We found no sign in any place:

And soon again stood face to face
Before the gaping door:
And stole into the room once more
As frighten'd children steal [...]

We seem'd to stand for an endless while,
Though still no word was said,
Three men alive on Flannan Isle,
Who thought on three men dead.

SUTHERLAND

✧ Ardvreck Castle ✧ – legends fae Loch Assynt

The ruined tower-house of Ardvreck Castle stands on the shores of Loch Assynt. It was built in the sixteenth century by Macleod of Assynt, possibly around 1590.

In 1672, the castle was attacked and overwhelmed by the Mackenzies. They took possession of the surrounding lands, and in 1726, built a more comfortable residence beside the Calda Burn and named it Calda House. The house did not stand for long; it was razed to the ground in 1737.

The impressive ruins of Ardvreck Castle make a beautiful foreground to this landscape. Both the remains of the castle and the house can be visited with care.

In 1890, Sir John Sinclair reportedly wrote, 'It was without a doubt the scene of "Many a wassail wild and deed of blood"; but now there is not a cat to mew nor a cock to crow, in the fortress of the Clan Macleod.'

There are a number of tales concerning the founding of the castle and the reason for its premature demise. Bob Pegg recently recorded a version of one of the legends in his book Highland Folk Tales. *Essie Stewart assisted me with the first tale and told me the other two stories. Essie is one of the Gaelic travellers and storytellers from this area, who gathered stories from her grandfather.*

Thanks to Essie for her time and willingness to allow me to tell these tales. As you read these legends, you will have to decide what is truth and what has built up around it. GB

✧ The Old Woman of Ardvreck ✧

As soon as I began to speak to Essie about the following story, she remarked, oh yes, the wicked woman at Ardvreck! She would whip up storms on Loch Assynt; the road to Kylesku would be bathed in sunshine, but Loch Assynt would be boiling with rough waves. It was wonderful to have Essie tell her thoughts of this woman, which are included in the tale below.

Many years ago, before a castle ever stood on the shore of Loch Assynt, there lived a wicked old woman who relished setting neighbour against neighbour. She would cause upset and grief wherever she could. Of a morning, this ordinary wee woman, with her black skirt and snow-white mutch, would be feeding her hens when she would see someone fishing the loch. If it was a man she disliked, she would murmur under her breath, stirring up a storm on the water, and cause the wee boat to struggle and perhaps flip over, drowning the occupant within. Such were the evil deeds of this witch.

One year, the woman had noticed that a local farmer had taken a pretty young wife. The witch watched each day as the young husband diligently rose early to feed the beasts and work his land. In the summer, he had to journey into the hills to take the beasts to high pasture. The husband was away for some weeks and during this time the old woman saw a male visitor come regularly to see the young wife.

Sure enough, some months on, the old woman noticed the young wife was blossoming with child, and decided it was her business to drop hints to the husband that this child was not his own. She did it slyly; she did it well.

'Good morning!' she said to the farmer, 'and how is your wife?'

'Mornin',' the man replied warily. There was always ill intent when the Ardvreck wife gave you the time of day.

'Your wife is looking very well. She is with child?'

The husband looked confused.

'Oh!' the wicked woman exclaimed, 'you did not know? She is at least four months gone, I would say. I think she must have came with child when you were away at the shieling ...'

She chattered on, watching through narrowed eyes as the implication of what she had said began to penetrate this good, simple man's mind. The man turned away from the old woman, his face pale and set, his shoulders slumped.

That night there were strong words spoken in the couple's wee home, and when the bairn was born, the husband knew he was not the father. In his grief, he was at the point of murdering both mother and child. Weeping, his young wife pleaded with him to allow her brothers to come, that she might prove her innocence. Reluctantly, he agreed, and both brothers were summoned.

The younger brother had recently returned from studying the dark arts in Italy. It was this brother that insisted they confront the accuser, the old woman of Ardvreck. She agreed to this arrangement. The following day, they arrived at her dwelling.

'Now old woman, let us put your accusation to the test. We will summon a mutual acquaintance to see the truth of what you say!'

The old woman nodded her acceptance, a glint in her eye. The young man knelt to the floor, and with a finger, began to draw symbols and letters of unknown form and shape, while muttering in a foreign tongue. Although the day had been calm and clear, suddenly the waters of the loch could be heard surging outside. Great waters began to writhe, and a devilish mist rose and pervaded the land and the sky above.

'Now,' called the brother to the husband, 'see the person I have called!'

The simple farmer fearfully turned to see the shadow of a figure standing at the wall. He gasped, terrified.

'Speak to him! Now!' cried his brother-in-law. 'While he remains!'

Reluctantly, the farmer turned to the shadowy figure, and raising his head, asked quietly, 'Is the child my bairn?'

The black figure seemed to darken, then slowly shook its head. As it did, a huge wave rose from the surface of the loch and crashed against the house, gushing through the windows and flooding the floor, while tearing at the roof. The heavens opened, and wind and rain lashed against the thick walls, and the floor seemed to shift as if it was a ship at sea.

The condemned wife was out of her wits with fear, and cried out in grief and remorse, but even in his terror, the cuckold husband would not go near his wife to comfort her.

'The Devil needs his gift, old woman!' cried out the brother. 'He will not leave until he receives it! Who can you spare?'

As the floor heaved beneath her feet, the pale old woman silently turned round; hiding in a corner, a wee lass was cowering. The old woman beckoned her to come; the lass rushed over to the old woman and clung to her skirts, screaming with terror.

'Here!' shouted the old woman. 'She's just an orphan! She will do!'

A commanding voice spoke over the tumult. It was the summoned figure. 'No! Not her. She is baptised; I cannot take her!'

At that, another huge wave engulfed the dwelling, filling it with water and almost drowning those within.

'Take the old woman!' screamed the older brother desperately, struggling for a footing as the room swam with water.

'No, she is mine already! It is not her time. No! I will take that which shall be missed and grieved for most!' And at once the shadow vanished.

Immediately, the loch ceased to writhe and was restored to its calm; the clouds dispersed, and the moon rose peacefully over the ruined house. The walls were bowed in, the roof had been badly damaged, and the old woman cursed as she looked round at the destruction.

When the farmer and his wife returned to their home, darkness had gone before them; the young baby was dead.

It is said that for some years following this dabbling with the Devil, the land was wasted. No healthy crops would grow – every grain was shrivelled and blackened – and the lochs were empty of good fish.

Five years later, there was a fire in the old woman's dwelling, which quickly rose up, and none could quench the flames. The house was razed to the ground, and no one knew how the fire had begun. The old witch was burned to death, and from that time the land was restored. The crops were healthy and abundant, and the lochs were once again teeming with life.

Whether the farmer and his wife remained as man and wife is not told.

✧ In Pursuit of Status ✧

The Chief of Macleod was not contented with his lot, and sadly his means of achieving his own ends were to have dire consequences.

Many years ago, Chief Macleod of Assynt lived simply in a small croft, for he had land, but there was no money. Seeing his poverty, other clan chiefs ridiculed him, mocking the fact that he had no grand dwelling to display his status. This rankled with the man, but there was nothing he could do. It happened one day that Satan came by while Macleod was sitting brooding in his croft. He greeted the chief, saying, 'I will give you money to build a home worthy of a man with your standing.' Macleod looked at the Devil suspiciously; there was never something given for nothing with the likes of him.

Satan smiled. 'I am quite happy to give you as much money as you need, but in return, I desire your daughter's hand in marriage. She is very beautiful!'

Macleod set his lips grimly and shook his head. That was not going to happen. Satan looked at him questioningly, acknowledged Macleod's response with a smile, and turned on his heel to leave.

Macleod was in turmoil, though. Here was an offer that would surely never come again. Before the Devil had gone much further, the chief blurted out, 'All right! I will take your offer!'

Satan nodded, satisfied. 'Very well, you shall have all the money you require to build your castle, and in one year, I will be back to claim my part of the bargain.'

On receiving the money, Macleod set about building his expansive castle. Completed, it was an impressive sight. Macleod hoped against hope that the Devil would forget his part of the bargain, and tried to put it out of his mind, making no mention of it to his beloved daughter. But a year to the day on which the bargain was struck, Satan appeared once more.

Macleod's daughter was told of her marriage to the tall, dark stranger she had just met, and not reluctantly, she became the stranger's bride. That night, as the newly wed couple mounted the stairs to their chamber, she happened to glimpse down, and saw, to her horror, that he had no feet, but cloven hooves instead. Rather than a fate with the Devil, the young woman mounted the stairs of the tower until she reached the battlements, and threw herself over. She was dashed to death on the rocks below.

It is said that if you walk the shore of Loch Assynt on a quiet summer's evening, you can still hear the daughter of Macleod weeping over her dreadful fate. Some say that the daughter, known as Eimhir, survived by diving into the waters of the loch, where she took up residence in the underwater caverns that permeate Loch Assynt. She transformed into a mermaid-like creature, which has been seen on the rocks that surround the loch. When Eimhir weeps at her fate, she causes the waters to rise and thresh in a violent manner.

As for the Devil, he was so furious at losing his prize, it is said he invoked a dreadful curse. Huge boulders rained down from the mountains, obliterating the lands of Macleod. The rock-strewn hillsides and landscape are still visible at Inchnadamph.

✧ An Inhospitable Welcome ✧

Essie had great respect for Sir James Graham, and was well impressed with his brave demeanour. But as for the Macleods, she felt the clan was cursed by their actions.

Another tale involving Macleod of Ardvreck is set in 1650. James Graham, also known as the Great Montrose, was defeated at the Battle of Carbisdale and fled for his life. He knew where he was headed. He was confident that Clan Chief Neil Macleod would give him refuge at Ardvreck Castle. Neil was the great grandson of the Macleod who had built the castle.

Battle weary, hungry and despondent, Graham arrived at Macleod's door. Neil was away on clan business, but his wife Christina warmly welcomed the fugitive. As soon as the door was shut behind him, Graham was seized, clapped in irons and imprisoned in the castle's dungeon.

As soon as it was convenient, he was transferred, first to Inverness, and then to Edinburgh. When it came time for his execution, Graham appeared before the masses, dressed in beautiful garments. As he mounted the steps to the gallows, the hangman asked, 'Have you any last request, sir?'

'Indeed,' said Montrose. 'May I put on my gloves?'

The hangman assented, and watched as the gentleman calmly took out a pair of white kid gloves and slipped them on, as if about to enter his carriage.

Then this dapper man was hanged.

✧ The Bark is Worse than the Bite ✧ – a legend fae Achiltibuie

Achiltibuie is one of my favourite places in Scotland, and not far from it stands Stac Pollaidh, the first mountain that I ever climbed, at the age of 5! I spent many camping holidays by the sands of Achnahaird, but I never knew of the following tale. Joan Gray, who was brought up in this beautiful area, heard this story from her uncle, Willie Macleod, and happily told it to me. GB

Long, long ago there lived a giant. One day, he and his wife found themselves in great danger; a pack of starving wolves had caught their blood scent and began to pursue them, howling madly. Terrified, the giant lifted his wife up on to his great back, tucked her legs under his arms and ran as fast as he could towards the pine forest.

By the time the giant reached the treeline with his precious load, the snarling pack was fast gaining on them. Exhausted and desperate, he had no choice but to plunge his way into the heavily forested wood, holding tightly to his wife. The giant laboured on, his head low, shoving his way through dark, densely packed branches. Gradually, the sound of pursuit began to fade. His breath was coming in great gasps now; his head and shoulders were torn, bruised and bleeding from battering his way through the almost unyielding forest. Yet the giant kept on.

After many hours, the trees began to thin out and soon the giant was out in the open once more. He stopped and knelt down, his chest heaving with exhaustion. The wood was quiet. There was no sight or sound of the wolves, and relieved, the giant prepared to help his wife down from his back. To his dismay, he suddenly realised he could not feel the weight of her on his back, all that remained were his wife's legs that had been tucked under his arms. Her head and torso were gone, cruelly ripped off by the branches in the forest that he had crashed through, and now were nowhere to be seen.

Broken-hearted, the giant tossed his wife's legs as far as he possibly could, and where they landed, a loch formed.

Today, if you go up Stac Pollaidh and look down, you will see the expanse of Loch Lurgainn below. If you look carefully, you will see the loch is in the shape of two legs twisted away from one another.

✧ A Cave o' Dark Deeds ✧ – legends fae Smoo Cave

Many strange myths are told of Smoo Cave near Durness. It was known to be a smuggler's den, but many speak of its supernatural qualities. At one time it was said to be the home of the spirits who stood guard to the underworld. SB

Devilish Ways

Donald Mackay, chief of Clan Mackay, Lord Reay, was reputed to have met with the Devil in Smoo Cave many times, but always managed to evade him. On one occasion the Devil followed Mackay to Durness, and then raced on ahead, trying to entrap him before he reached Smoo Cave. When the chief arrived, he sensed danger and sent his hound into the dark cave before him. Moments later, the poor beast limped out hairless, howling in terror and pain. Realising that great ill lay there, Mackay hung back until the sunrise, at which time the Devil had no power. The Evil One escaped the dawn by blasting through the roof of the cave, creating three gaping holes, which are still evident to this day.

Stash

In the sixteenth century a feared robber and murderer called McMurdo threw his victims down Smoo Cave's blowhole. He is buried at Balnakeil church.

Refuge

On one occasion Smoo Cave saved the folk of Durness. Clan Gunn had crossed the borders of Sutherland intent on raiding and killing the folk of the district. The locals pretended to flee from their enemies, and ran into the cave, followed closely by the Gunn clansmen. The locals knew the caves well and hid amongst the nooks and crannies; when their enemy approached they killed their attackers until all the invading clansmen were dead.

Deathly Trick

Smoo Cave occasionally enjoyed aiding and abetting adventurers. Soon after the 1745 rebellion, two excise officers were tasked with locating and destroying all illicit whisky stills around Durness. Donald Mackay's still was deep within the cave, but he accepted a bribe to lead the two excise men to its source. The tide was rising and the cave could only be accessed by boat. The waves were becoming increasingly stormy and angry as they entered the cave and the excise men were naturally terrified. Mackay deliberately capsized the boat; being a strong swimmer he could withstand the ferocity of the tide and swam for shore safely, but the other two men were drowned. One body was washed up along the coast, the other was never found.

To this day, when the tide runs high, the excise man's ghost appears inside the inner chamber of Smoo Cave, exactly where the boat was overturned.

ORKNEY

✧ The Great Serpent of the North ✧ – the legend o' Assipattle and the Stoorworm

Some people have questioning minds, and seek to know how things came to be. Legends were and still are a way of explaining the unknown, and can take on all different forms. In this particular tale, we meet a sea monster that would have huge geographical implications! GB

Many years ago in the Kingdom of Orkney, there lived a family with many children – plenty of boys, but just one daughter. The youngest lad was lazy, and spent most of his days lying about in the ash pit while his brothers worked the land with their father. When they returned from work, they would torment their brother for his idleness, and they called him Assipattle. His only friend was his sister, who would play with him and listen to his inventive and colourful stories, of which there were many.

One day, the king's daughter passed by with her escort and caught sight of Assipattle's sister. She requested that the lass come to be her maid at the palace. This was a great honour, and although sad to leave her family, especially her little brother, the sister agreed.

At that time a huge serpent-like creature came to the shores of the kingdom and began to create havoc, wrecking crops and stealing cattle with its long forked tongue. The king sent his soldiers out to try to vanquish the beast but many died from the blast of poisonous fumes that spewed from its mouth.

The creature was known as the stoorworm. To appease the monster and stave off its destructive tendencies for a time, it was given a regular supply of human food, the flesh of seven young beautiful maidens every Saturday. Unfortunately there was a limited supply of such delicacies and there came a day when the king knew that unless he did something soon, his only daughter would have to be sacrificed too.

In great distress, Assipattle's sister came running back home in tears, explaining that her princess would die unless a brave knight vanquished the stoorworm! The king had offered a reward to any valiant young man who would accomplish this deed. But no one had the courage to face such a dreadful serpent, so the king, although old in years, was going to attack the stoorworm himself the very next day, in an attempt to prevent his daughter from being sacrificed.

Assipattle stood up in his rags, covered in ashes. 'I will kill the stoorworm!' he said stoutly.

His brothers burst out laughing; what had Assipattle ever accomplished?

From all over the land people were planning to gather the next day to see the king face the stoorworm with his great sword, Sicklesnapper, which had once belonged to Odin. If he died, they would have to watch the princess being devoured too, and then what would happen?

All the citizens of the country were preparing to attend the spectacle, all except Assipattle; his father had told him he must stay behind. Assipattle knew in his heart he had the courage to kill the stoorworm, but how was he to find the means of getting there before the king?

That night, Assipattle overheard his parents talking about their journey the following day; his mother could not walk that far and his father offered to let her ride with him.

'My dear,' said the wife, 'how is it that if anyone else rides your horse, it is as slow as an old nag but when you ride her, you make her go as fast as the wind?'

'I have a secret,' said her husband. 'To make my mare bide still, I clap her on her left shoulder, to make her trot like any other horse, I clap her twice on the right shoulder, but if I whistle through a goose thrapple[6] into her ear, my horse has to fly! So I always keep a goose's thrapple in my coat pocket.'

On hearing this Assipattle smiled. He went straight to where the thrapple had been hidden and taking it, headed out to the stable. He saddled the mare and following his father's instructions, he was soon flying along like the wind.

Even so, dawn was breaking as he approached the coast. He looked down to the water and saw the huge dark shape of the monster sprawled across the bay. Tying up the mare, he made his way down the cliff to where he saw a small cottage. He knocked, but there was no reply. Quietly he went in and saw an old woman asleep. He tiptoed around until he saw what he was after, a clay pot. He lifted a glowing peat from the fire and whispering his apologies to the sleeping woman, he went out of the door and down to the beach.

The king's boat was anchored just off the shore guarded by one faithful soldier. 'Who goes there?' the man shouted.

'Just down looking for mussels for breakfast,' called Assipattle. 'Would you like to come and share some with me?'

'Ach laddie!' laughed the soldier. 'You canna trick me intae comin ashore like that! I'd hae my head cut off for disobeyin' the King!'

Assipattle shrugged, and turned to the rocks to pick off a few shells; then he began to dig in the sand to make a fire. Suddenly he stopped and exclaimed, 'Gold! I've found gold!' He made a great

6 Windpipe.

show of digging deeper in a very excited manner. This was too much for the soldier; he brought the boat in, hauled it up onto the sand, and pushing Assipattle aside, he began to dig for himself.

Assipattle sidled over to the boat with his clay pot, pushed it off the sand, jumped aboard and by the time the soldier realised he had been tricked, Assipattle was too far out to be caught.

With no real plan, Assipattle rowed towards the stoorworm. Its head was facing in his direction; it was sleeping. The lad noticed that every time the worm breathed in, gallons of water were swallowed down into its gullet and then poured out of its gills.

Taking a deep breath, he steered the little boat straight towards its gaping mouth and suddenly found himself washed into its dark, cavernous jaws and down into the belly of the beast, which became drier and darker the deeper he went. Eventually the boat would go no further and lifting up the clay pot with the glowing peat as a light, he continued down into the very belly of the serpent. There, towering over the lad's head was the stoorworm's huge, glistening liver and suddenly Assipattle knew what he must do. Taking the peat he thrust it deep into the centre of the liver and turning round he scrabbled back and into his boat. Just in time!

The stoorworm's body went into spasm as it tried to rid itself of the sudden excruciating pain. As it did, the boat was forcefully propelled up through the worm, out of its mouth and straight into the air. It soared over the water until it smacked down onto the beach in front of an outraged king. He was standing there with his sword and all his retinue, who all gaped open-mouthed at Assipattle and his flying boat. There was no time for the king to be furious that his boat had been stolen for now all eyes were turned to the tortured stoorworm. It was creating huge waves, screaming and thrashing about the bay, as it desperately tried to rid itself of the agonising torment within.

It lashed out with its head and its long forked tongue flew out of its mouth and sailed through the sky until it crashed down fracturing the Nordic lands almost in two. Water rushed in to form narrow straits between the divide, separating what is now called Denmark from the countries of Norway and Sweden.

As the serpent continued violently threshing around, teeth flew out from its mouth and formed, firstly, the string of islands known as the Shetland Isles and then, further north and west the Faroe Islands.

In its death throes the stoorworm curled in on itself and became a mound, and from that day to this, it has forever smoked in its centre. This large island became known as Iceland.

The king was greatly relieved not to have to fight the worm and was delighted it had been vanquished. Despite Assipattle's ragged and sooty appearance, he honoured the brave young man, giving him his faithful sword Sicklesnapper and his daughter's hand in marriage. So in time, Assipattle became king and reigned wisely and long, loved by all his people.

And that is how many of the lands of the north were formed.

SHETLAND

✧ Field of Blood ✧

History and superstition often go hand in hand. Across this country and across the world, there have been dreadful deeds committed in the name of a higher cause, where hatred, fear and rage spew out and taint the land, and it is as if the ground remembers. Many years ago, I heard the traveller Stanley Robertson tell a tale about a field of blood. GB

The field had seen so many bloody feuds and conflicts that it had become a feared and dreaded place where none would tread. It was so steeped in blood that nothing of use would grow, and instead the land had turned a sickly red colour, and from the earth there grew up deadly, bloodthirsty ivy-like vines. For the unsuspecting traveller, to walk upon the land was fatal, for the vines would snake out thorn-studded tendrils which would seize the person and grip them by the ankles; the cruel thorns would penetrate the skin, poisoning their victim, while allowing the ferocious plants to slake their thirst on the unfortunate's blood.

For many years, few chose to venture here, and even fewer lived close by; the field and the surrounding area were left abandoned, and the whole region was affected by it. However, one day, an unsuspecting priest was passing through, and came to the neglected field. Not knowing the danger, he decided to shorten his journey by crossing it.

As he stepped into the field, the blood-parched vines silently rose up all around and attacked him. The priest screamed out in terror, but fortunately, some labourers who were harvesting in the neighbouring fields heard his cries and came running. With little thought to their own safety, the men ran into the field scything down the carnivorous plants as they made their way towards the poor priest, who could hardly be seen beneath a writhing, seething mass of green. With yells of fury, the men tore the priest out from the clutches of the vines and dragged his body to safety, but blood was pouring from the man's many wounds.

The labourers hurriedly took the desperately ill man to the nearest dwelling, where a wise woman known as a spey wife lived. She knew exactly what to do. Taking powdered leaves of yarrow and slippery elm, she made up a balm, which she spread over the priest's wounds to staunch the bleeding. Although he was barely conscious, she forced him to drink down a pottage to help draw out the poison.

It took many days for the priest to recover, but he was in good hands, and as he was nursed back to health he learnt much from the old woman. When he had finally regained his strength, he respectfully asked that there might be a gathering of all the people who lived nearby. This was an unusual request, but out of curiosity, the locals agreed to meet together with the priest.

With all the people gathered, the priest humbly thanked the spey wife for her wisdom and care, and also expressed his gratitude to the men who had rescued him from certain death. He explained that he and the spey wife had discussed how best to rid the parish of this evil. He suggested to the people that the land had been cursed and could only be assuaged by blood, but why not the blood of creatures rather than that of men and women? At slaughtering time, why not empty buckets of blood onto the field to quench its seemingly endless thirst? He also suggested a purging, with prayers and holy water. The people were relieved that here at last was a priest willing to help them and they agreed to carry out his ideas.

And so it was that the following week, the community gathered around the field with buckets filled with beasts' blood and vessels of holy water. The blood was poured out and the vines swarmed out of the ground to devour it. Then prayers were cried out, hymns were sung and holy water spread onto the cursed ground. The people watched as the vines reared and writhed and then shrivelled into nothing. Immediately, the earth began to turn a rich black colour and, as they watched, thin green shoots began to sprout from the soil.

After so long, the ground had at last been healed.

Still Today ...

In Shetland, there are areas of land regarded as cursed by war. Years ago, the island of Unst was invaded by Norsemen, and many natives were put to the sword, though it was not entirely one-sided.

One day some time later, at the site of one of these battles in Swineness, a man saw no reason not to plough and plant the soil. It seemed rich and he was sure there would be a good harvest. But when he came to reap his crop, blood flowed from each one of the stems and salt tears fell from the ears of corn.

In Burrafjord and by Norwick, the areas of land where battles were fought are known as the fields of the dead. No person had ever worked the soil in these places, for it was believed that if they did, a curse would fall upon them or those near and dear to them.

In one of these fields, a woman defied this superstition and began to dig the ground. Not long after this, her favourite cow keeled over and died. Undeterred, the following year she grimly returned to the same piece of ground to prepare the soil for planting, and then she sowed corn. But it was costly – her husband took ill and died. From that day on, the land has remained fallow.

✧ Wulvers ✧

When I was up north I met a young Shetland fiddler who had been playing at a folk session in a nearby venue. With very little prompting, he treated me to a Shetland story of the Wulver, half wolf, half man. Not all Scots werewolves are sinister, he assured me! SB

The wulvers of Shetland have the head of a wolf, but a man's body covered in brown, short hair. Usually they are to be encountered sitting on a rock fishing, and occasionally they will leave any uneaten fish on the window ledges of poor islanders. Some Shetland people associate the wulver with ancient burial grounds or ruined buildings. Others believe that to see a wulver is an indication of impending death. They are even reported to have been seen sitting near to the house where a person lay dying.

INVERNESS

✧ The Loch Ness Monster and Other Tales ✧ – legends fae Loch Ness to Lochaber

From when I was a child until quite recently, the Loch Ness Monster had been a familiar story or curio that probably compares with the fairies I imagined in the birch wood near my childhood home in Lenzie.

Our family often met tourists who were 'doing' a one-day tour of Scotland. Many were intent on including Loch Ness in their itinerary so that they might catch a glimpse of the Loch Ness Monster. Our eyes would roll, but we would not disappoint them but regale them with tales in which we ourselves held no belief. However, over the years I have become increasingly aware that this creature is not so easy to dismiss as legend or myth.

Loch Ness has many inflows from the surrounding mountains. The water is murky as a result of the peaty surrounds, making visibility underwater very poor. Recently I spoke to an open-water swimmer who said that when he swam in the loch he could not see his arms under the water because it was so full of minute peat debris. Such an environment could be a wonderful hiding place for amphibians of many sizes.

Trawling through material about the 'Loch Ness Monster', there is one thing of which I am sure. You must decide for yourself, on the evidence presented, as to whether it proves the existence of an unusual creature, or creatures, dwelling in Loch Ness, or not. GB

Ancient Sightings

The first recorded sighting of a large, unknown creature in the vicinity of Loch Ness is in an account from the seventh century, written by the monk Adamnan. The text gives the following account.

The now-famous Columba and his party were travelling west and saw a burial taking place by the River Ness. While swimming, an unfortunate man had been mauled to death by some kind of aquatic beast. In order to cross the river, the travellers required the ferry that was on the opposite bank, so Columba asked one of his followers to swim across to fetch it. Thereupon, the dreadful creature reappeared, intent on attacking the swimmer, but Columba made the sign of the cross and ordered the monster away, and it fled in terror.

Superstitious and Frightening

For many Highlanders, if they saw an unusual creature emerging from, or seen by the water, it could be dangerous and was to be avoided at all costs, especially if it was horse-shaped. Until relatively recent times, there were places people would avoid, because of previous incidents in that area. The general consensus was that such a beast would have evil intent, although it might at first appear docile.[7]

According to a descendant of Mr James Macgrigor, his ancestor had a confrontation with a kelpie on the road between Strathspey and Inverness. The creature was known to entice travellers to mount its saddle and then dive into the water with its prey. These people were never seen alive again. On this particular night, the kelpie saw a man

---

7 Through the centuries, there have been many tales of kelpies, water horses, water bulls and other such aquatic beasts. Roland Watson in his book *The Water Horses of Loch Ness* thoroughly examines these legends and the vivid accounts of personal encounters with these creatures. It is a fascinating read.

approaching, and began to prepare to dupe its next victim. As soon as Macgrigor saw the kelpie, he was determined to destroy it. He marched up, drew his sword and smote it mightily across its nose. The kelpie fell, and the bridle around its head broke; the bit fell out of the creature's mouth and landed on the ground.

Macgrigor picked the bit up as the kelpie struggled to rise; it was shocked at the outcome of the encounter, and in considerable pain. Macgrigor watched the kelpie warily; he was prepared for retaliation, and was surprised when the kelpie asked him humbly to return the bit he had in his hand. Immediately the man asked, 'I can return the bit to you, but first, tell me, why? What is it to you?'

The creature replied, 'As a messenger of the dark, it gifts me with supernatural strength, so that I would have thrashed you near to death! Without it, I am weak. I have been robbed of my strength, and by the morrow I will be dead! The bit is magical, for through the holes of this bit you can see all that is fey and unseen to the human eye – it gives the second sight.'

'Hmmm,' mused Macgrigor, 'I do not think I will return this bit to you.' With that, he began to run for home. The kelpie was furious and tried to prevent Macgrigor from entering his house, but it was held in check by the rowan branch on the front door. The man threw the bit up to his wife, who was watching at the window. Knowing it was defeated the kelpie retreated, never to be seen again. As for Macgrigor, equipped with this supernatural bit, he became renowned locally as the Warlock.

More Recent Sightings

Since the 1930s, many sightings of the Loch Ness Monster have been recorded, whereas before this, word of mouth sufficed. It is said that for every sighting of 'Nessie' recorded by the media, there are many more; locals often see her as they go about their daily business without making an issue of it.

In a letter from the chief constable of Inverness Constabulary to the Under-Secretary of State dated 15 August 1938, the chief constable was concerned about trophy hunters travelling to the loch with the specific intent of killing 'Nessie'. It states, 'That there is some strange creature in Loch Ness seems now beyond doubt.'

To explore Loch Ness for signs of an aquatic creature requires dedication and endurance. It is surely no easy task, and can be costly in many ways, not least time.

Many people attempt to discredit claims of a 'Loch Ness Monster' sighting; they might discount it and say the sighting was of a log, or a boat's displacement wave, or fish, seals, sharks, or rocks. While this may often be true, is it always the case?

In April 2013, a Loch Ness Monster Symposium was held in Edinburgh. A number of speakers gave talks, followed by a panel discussion on 'Nessie'. When asked, the audience was divided 50/50 as to her existence. Only one out of the four speakers expressed his outright belief in a 'resident amphibious-like fish', and only one stated emphatically that there was nothing there.

Over the years, there have been numerous accounts and photographs attributed to sightings of the Loch Ness Monster. In amongst those who are genuinely convinced they have seen the creature on the loch, there are 'hoaxters' and opportunists who have taken advantage of a public willing to believe, and have capitalised on this. For some this has discredited all evidence.

There are many websites, books and paraphernalia associated with the creature and its controversy. Some of these give fair exposure to the believers and the sceptics.

Here I describe just a few of the sightings that have been recorded more recently.

In 1933, a wife and husband were travelling up Loch Ness-side. As her husband drove, the woman witnessed a commotion on the water, and two dark humps appeared, both of which were 6 to 7 feet in diameter. They remained above the surface for about a minute, moving at great speed towards the shore, then swerved and sank underwater. This was followed by a powerful wave that crashed ashore on the otherwise calm surface. As an avid angler who was accustomed to recognising wildlife, the woman discounted the possibility of the creature being a large seal, or any other animal with which she was acquainted.

A recent account involved a man who spent three years searching the loch for 'Nessie' with sonar, clocking up many miles in the process. While out in his boat in September 2011, he recorded sonar hits of three, large, unidentified objects in one area. He retraced his movements several hours later, but no contact was made on sonar, indicating that the objects were no longer there; they had been on the move.

In August 2013, there was a sighting of 'Nessie' near Fort Augustus. While a man was photographing a swan, he glimpsed a peculiar movement of water. His description was of a 15-foot-long black object moving just below the surface, which caused the water to flow over it like a wave. He stated there was no other boat activity close by on the loch at that time. The account was reported in a sensational fashion by several newspapers, accompanied by one of his pictures.

And Further Afield

Southwest of Loch Ness is the deepest expanse of freshwater in the British Isles, Loch Morar. In contrast to Loch Ness, the waters of this loch are crystal clear. Here too there have been sightings of an unidentified creature, more entangled with legend than 'Nessie'. When 'Morag' was seen, locals often regarded it as a forewarning of death. If her weeping and wailing were heard, it caused dismay, being the harbinger of doom. In accounts dating back to the nineteenth century, she was described in two ways; first as looking like a moving, water-logged boat, second as a mythical creature with a woman's head and torso with fish-like body and tail.

Back in August 1969, two men were out in their small motorboat for an evening's fishing. It was still light when the men glanced behind them and saw a large object moving at speed towards their vessel. It cannoned into them, rocking the boat dangerously. The men panicked. One, fearful they would capsize, took an oar and tried to thrust the creature away. The other went to turn off the engine, and turned back to see his friend struggling to fend off the huge creature with the oar. He reached for his rifle and shot, and at once the aquatic beast disappeared below the surface.[8]

In August 2013, a couple saw Morag three times during their two-day visit to Loch Morar. The man was a recently retired oil engineer, not known for his imaginative wanderings. He asked the B&B owner if there were any rocks visible at the surface in the middle of the loch. His host laughed, saying no, how could there be? The loch was almost 1,000 feet deep. The creature was described as being submarine-like in shape and size. The onlookers were able to watch it for a long time.

Around the same time, a local man had been out in his boat fishing with a number of other people, and not 50 yards away they had seen three humps rising from the water moving through the loch. It was an unsettling sight!

From a Personal View

As I step gingerly down the slippery path to the loch's edge, anticipation floods through me. I look out eagerly, smiling at the excitement I feel. Just maybe there will be a glimpse?

The loch is calm, slight ripples gently stroke the shore and I see reflections in the glass stillness. Not a bird, not a splash as I gaze the length of this

8 Dr Donald Stewart from the University of Edinburgh is quoted saying, 'Clearly there is something going on in Loch Morar, whatever it is.'

seemingly endless stretch of water. What kind of luck does it take to be in exactly the right place at the right time with camera poised to capture this elusive creature?

The mighty Loch Ness is over twenty-two miles long, over a mile wide and more than 750 feet deep. In fact, the loch is more voluminous than all the lakes in England and Wales combined. Finding any creature on or in a body of water of this size is like trying to find the proverbial needle in a haystack.

I had a friend, Ina Ross, whom I greatly respected; she died a few years ago. She used to live with her family in Glengarry in Lochaber, not far from Loch Ness. I remember her telling me about the day she and her husband stopped at Urquhart Castle, which overlooks one of the deepest areas of the loch. She told me about their sighting of the monster as a matter of fact; they had seen two humps visible in the water. I remember I smiled and nodded in a jokey manner, but was stymied by the truth that Ina was not making this up, and that this was, of course, what she had seen.

For me, that is enough, I for one am convinced!

✧ In the Wrong Camp ✧ – urban myths and legends fae Lochalsh tae Culloden

I was chatting to my friend Pat on the phone one day and telling her about the book I was writing and she remembered an incident that had happened to her some years previously. Pat agreed that I could share her experience with you. GB

During the summer some years ago, my friend Pat and her friend John travelled north for a camping weekend. It was glorious weather and they enjoyed the journey, pottering along and exploring rivers en route. Eventually they arrived at an unknown lovely spot close to a river and set up camp. They made food and began to settle down to sleep.

In the middle of the night Pat was suddenly woken by angry voices close to the tent. Blinking in the dark, she strained to try to discern words, but Pat could not hear what was being said. Yet she was gripped by a fear and an oppressive sense of violent danger, convinced that she and her partner were about to be hurt badly. The aggressive voices seemed to be coming closer; they were furiously shouting. Pat gripped her sleeping bag tightly around her; she heard metal scraping horribly against metal. It seemed very close. Terrified, Pat saw and felt the tent begin to move.

She woke up John, who seemed unworried; he could not hear any voices but he did see the tent being pushed inwards. Pat's driving panic shouted at her to escape and John's inability to grasp the danger began to make her hysterical. John tried in vain to calm Pat down. In a reassuring manner John suggested there was probably an animal like a sheep or cow outside the tent. He unzipped the front flap but nothing was to be seen or heard on the landscape surrounding them.

The silence seemed loud, and to Pat the darkness was oppressive. John took the torch and went around the tent to have a good look but came back puzzled. He shook his head and tried to laugh the whole thing off but Pat could not calm back down. She was unable to push away a sense of impending doom; it felt malevolent. Pat was so agitated and unsettled that she implored John to leave everything and get back to the car as quickly as possible. Exasperated, he tried to argue that there was nothing wrong and everything was fine, but Pat would not be persuaded. Eventually, rather disgruntled, John took Pat back to the car and they drove out of the glen. They found a pub car park some distance away and made the best of sleeping there for the rest of the night.

When they were driving back to the glen in the morning, Pat still felt ill at ease. She told John that under no circumstances would she spend another night in the place. They parked in a layby and got out of the car. Just beyond them they noticed an interpretation board. Curious, they both went to look at where exactly they were.

As she read the information a cold shiver ran up Pat's spine; it was an account of the Battle of Glen Shiel that had taken place on the very spot where they had been camping on 10 June 1719. The previous day had been 10 June.

John needed no further persuasion; they packed up their tent and belongings and headed for home.

Still to this day, when recounting the tale, Pat is reminded of the overwhelming terror that she knew that night. It was as if the veil of time had been removed to transport her back to the very day the battle took place, and experience the horror and fear of war.

✧ An Account of the Battle of Glen Shiel ✧

At the beginning of the eighteenth century, the Jacobites were seeking to make another stand against the Hanoverian crown. Secret treaties with Spain were made; an armada was on its way. The plan was for the majority of the Spanish army to attack from Wales, while a token force would land in Scotland to support the rise and gathering of the clans as an army. A mustering of soldiers would begin at Eilean Donan Castle and on into Loch Duich and down Glen Shiel, and from there they would travel south.

A number of frigates arrived off the West coast with a force of Spanish disciplined infantry but unfortunately the English had pursued the ships into the mouth of Loch Duich and the majority of the Spanish soldiers were captured. In the south, the main fleet of the Spanish armada was overcome by a storm, some of the ships were swept onto enemy shores and many others were scattered.

When news came of the Spanish disaster, adjusted plans were made to attack Inverness; some of the clans had already gathered in Glen Shiel along with the remaining two hundred men from the Regiment of Galicia who had not been captured. The soldiers were hopeful of further reinforcements and chose to await their arrival. The men had good and bountiful weapons; they were confident of success.

When word came to Inverness of another Jacobite uprising, the English army led by General Wightman decided not to wait for the enemy to be reinforced and thus completely outnumber his troops; instead his soldiers would take the offensive.

On 7 June the eighteen-hundred-strong Jacobite army had word that the enemy was approaching Glen Shiel. Plans and preparations were made. By the following day the Jacobite supporters were in position, awaiting the arrival of the enemy forces.

It took till 5 p.m. for the English to complete their prepared offensive, which involved dragging in their artillery including many little mortars. These effective weapons proved to be very destructive to the clansman. The highlanders were positioned strategically on high ground to attack the troops below; they had been prepared for close hand-to-hand combat. Instead they became sitting ducks, blasted by overhead grenades.

By his careful assessment of his enemy, Wightman managed to outmanoeuvre the distracted clansmen with his troops. Although many of the Jacobites fought bravely, others on seeing defeat was inevitable, disappeared into the misty night.

The Galician troops were stymied in their centre-ground position; all support cover from each side was blasted, engaged or gone. By the following morning these brave allies had to surrender and were taken prisoner.

One enterprising band of Scotsmen blew up the remaining weapons; then scurried back to their glen before their presence could be missed and accusations of treason could be made.

At the end of the battle, the dead were left strewn in the glen, one hundred Jacobites and only twenty-one of their enemy.

✧ Culloden ✧

Other significant battles have taken place all around Scotland, but the most infamous of all is that of Culloden, the last stand of the Jacobite rebellion against Hanoverian rule.

Ghosts and Strange Happenings at Culloden

It is said that on the eve of battle, one Jacobite general, Lord George Murray, sighted a huge dark bird known as the Great Scree. For a superstitious people, it must have been a dreadful omen and was surely a harbinger of the doom that the following day brought to the country of Scotland. The consequences of this battle were far-reaching and affected the highland way of life forever.

The many Jacobites who were killed in battle were buried where they fell and it is said that every year on the anniversary of the battle, cries of battle and the clash of weapons can be heard. Some have seen sightings of single ghostly figures in highland dress, broken and weary of battle.

It is said that still, no bird will sing on the site of the battle or the area where the soldiers are buried; the land has had too much slaughter.

Many who visit the site of the Culloden battlefield are aware of sadness and a sense of mourning about the place.

A Brief Account of the Battle of Culloden and the Consequences for the Scottish People

It has to be understood that this battle was not so much about nationalism as about a people seeking to hold on to their religion and traditional way of life. For certain clan chiefs, they perceived change afoot and either sent their clansmen to fight on the Hanoverian side, or at least sent one son to fight on either side, so that they would not lose their lands. Thus, many Scots fought against Scots.

As with so many Scottish uprisings, success had been so close; the army had been led to within a hair's breadth of victory by their symbol of hope, Bonnie Prince Charlie. But unfortunate decision-making and disappointed clansmen led to the failure of the invasion of England.

The army retreated back to Scotland, and the Duke of Cumberland was determined to flatten the rebellion once and for all. Troops were stationed in Aberdeen. From there the army marched north, with a slow train of lethal weaponry in tow. The ominous sound of the heavy cannon being transported north could be heard for miles. When the Hanoverian army arrived at the chosen battlefield they were fed and rested and prepared to defeat the rebels completely.

The rallying and mobilising of deflated clans must have been a hard task; by the time the Jacobite army had been assembled, they were exhausted, soaked and starving. On 16 April 1746, the weather was dreadful. The chosen site for battle was a muddy, open moor with no cover or higher ground, not suitable for charging highlanders. The brave soldiers were given orders to charge and within forty minutes over one thousand men were dead. Although the rebel army retreated, there was to be no quarter given. Anyone with a hint of Jacobite about them was slaughtered, including those found harbouring fugitives.

Those who were captured were inevitably executed, and peers were beheaded. If a person spoke favourably of Prince Charlie, they would be imprisoned and deported. Clan life was prohibited; families were harried, dispersed and made homeless. Many cattle and sheep were taken or killed where they stood, robbing people of their livelihood and ensuring destitution.

The plaidie, or blanket, was standard clothing for the majority of people. It was a versatile length of cloth that doubled up as a blanket when unwound. It was now forbidden.

The Disarming Act was passed, forbidding any weapons, which included bagpipes. In fact a number of pipers were executed, as they were regarded as very effective offensive weapons!

WESTER AND EASTER ROSS

✧ Vicious Torture ✧ – a legend fae Kinlochewe

In many Scottish glens during the seventeenth century, families persistently continued to follow traditions that their forbears passed onto them. This included their oral history, their songs, stories, love of music and dance and their religious and often superstitious practices. The grip of the south began to be felt as the church began to demand adherence to certain laws and rules in order to guarantee the salvation of the soul. As the years passed, many rhythms and ways of life that singled glen folk out from other peoples were stamped on as being pagan, ungodly or of the Devil. Perhaps some of the old practices had been driven by fear, but the imposition of these new regulations was throwing the baby out with the bath water. A new kind of dread was established that shackled many, and is still felt: the fear of church reprisal.

I am very grateful to Liz Forrest from Kinlochewe for her help and advice in writing this story. Liz has researched the history of the churches in this area, and came across the following unhappy tale. GB

In the seventeenth century, Gairloch was still steeped in superstitious practices, which the Presbyterian Church could no longer tolerate. Bulls were still being sacrificed as a cure for lunacy, libations of milk poured out to please the gods and many of the locals were held in thrall to all this. The minister at that time seemed to have little influence on furthering the church's position in the area. But when the minister died, a man called Reverend John Morrison was called to the parish, and he was a very different fellow altogether. Unfortunately for Morrison, his appointment was not well received by John Mackenzie of Coul, who owned the lands of Kinlochewe and was the 'man with clout' in the area.

In March 1711, Morrison was inducted, but not locally in Gairloch; the excuse given was the inclement weather. A few days later Morrison arrived in the parish, fired up and eager to serve. But it was to be a bitter beginning.

Morrison began travelling around the parish to get to know his flock and the area. But when he reached Kinlochewe, he and his servant were waylaid. Their clothes were torn from their backs and the pair were imprisoned for three days in a shed filled with cattle and dung. The men were starved and given no comforts until the fourth morning.

On the fifth day, they were forcibly taken to the house of John Mackenzie, who made his dislike of Morrison very clear and swore that no Presbyterian minister would set foot on land that belonged to him unless he was forced to comply by Her Majesty's forces.

Despite numerous setbacks, the reverend was an uncommonly stubborn fellow and as spring turned to summer, he continued to preach the 'righteous way' with fervour wherever he could.

By late summer, Mackenzie's men had had enough, and they were determined to rid themselves of the preacher for good. On a hot, humid day when the skies were overcast and leaden with rain, they seized Morrison as he travelled by Letterewe on the east side of Loch Maree. The party stripped him of all his clothes and tied him to a tree, leaving him for the midges to feast upon. Imagine the torment! Every part of Morrison's outer anatomy was exposed to those little, black demon biters. The poor man was dehydrated, demented and red raw by the time he was found. It was late evening when an old woman came across the minister and untied him. He was delirious, in agony and hardly able to stand.

This was too much for Morrison. He begged to be released from the parish, and was sent up to Sutherland for a time. But in the spring of 1713, he returned, on the behest of Mackenzie of Gruinard, who had built a church and asked that Morrison preach there, which he promised to do, once a year. The minister just wished to serve the community in the way he knew best, but the community would not allow it. He was constantly harassed when he tried to access his manse or its lands, and suffered badly because he was not able to grow food or tend to his animals. There was very little support from the Presbytery.

By the end of 1716, Morrison was a broken man. Every year cattle had ruined his crops, his own beasts had been spirited away and the manse robbed of all his worldly goods. He left and was given a parish in Easter Ross.

Kinlochewe lay vacant for five years, but when a minister was appointed in 1721, he seemed to be received and accepted by the locals. Perhaps a few years down the line, religious views had mellowed, and the time was now ripe for the Presbyterians to wield the Bible in the way they thought best.

✧ The Black Sail of Loch Maree ✧ – a legend fae Gairloch

Loch Maree is a peaceful place; as the weather sweeps in from east or west, its waters reflect the ever-changing skies. On this gentle loch stands the Isle Maree, where chapel remains can be seen amongst a grove of trees; the flora on this island is unchanged from days so long ago. Oaks still grow here, reminders of the days of pagan worship and holly, the Christian ward against evil. GB

Many years ago, the Norse Vikings ruled the lands of Gairloch. As is the way of occupation, some lived and married locally. Both natives and Vikings crossed to the Isle Maree to worship and receive advice from the wise old monk who lived in his solitary cell there. He was a man who spoke his mind and was well respected for it.

At this time, a young Viking prince by the name of Olaf roamed Gairloch. He was brave and fearless, to the point of recklessness. Olaf was a natural leader, and likeable, but his one weakness was his temper. It could flare up and become a vicious, destructive force; no good sense or reason could quell it.

In the summer months, Olaf and his followers lived on his great warship on Loch Ewe, always ready for war. In winter, when storms boiled the waters into a rage, the Vikings would camp on the islands close by the loch. Often Olaf sought out the hermit on Isle Maree; the solitude was a balm to him and the old monk's wise words brought him peace of mind.

One day while returning from the Isle, he passed by a group of women gathering seaweed on the shore. One young, beautiful maiden caught Olaf's eye, and he was immediately smitten, as was she! The passionate young warrior set about wooing the lass, but he was in a quandary, as he could not see how he could marry her and then continue to live amongst his men on the ship. He sought advice from the monk, who suggested that Olaf build a dwelling on Isle Maree, close by the chapel. It would be secluded, yet not too far from his men. Olaf was delighted with this idea and set about planning a simple home for himself and his betrothed.

What celebrations were had on the island that wedding day! Such music, singing and rejoicing; the bride was brimming over with joy to be united with her husband in such a beautiful place. Many were the happy gatherings in the wooded groves over the months, and the prince and princess grew to love each other more and more deeply, seeking out each other's company above all else.

Olaf was a warrior, and after a time, his companions grew restless and called upon their leader to take them off raiding. But the prince was reluctant to leave his beautiful wife; his heart was filled with such passion for his princess, and time after time he managed to dissuade his warriors.

Some time later word came that there was to be a gathering, known as a Thing; all leaders were expected to attend. Even a preoccupied new husband could not ignore this call, and reluctantly Olaf began to make preparations to depart.

The young couple did not want to be separated from one another. Olaf's princess tearfully expressed her fears that he might die in battle or become ill, and she would be left in torment, not knowing his fate.

Olaf pondered on his wife's words and came up with a plan. Sails were made in two colours: black and white. When his ship returned to Loch Maree, if all was well, he would raise the white flag, but if not, his men would raise the black. And his princess could do the same.

On the day of departure, the two young lovers clung to one another, desperately unhappy to let the other go.

As the princess watched the great warship disappear up the loch and out of view, she felt her heart had been torn apart. Olaf was sad and sore to have to leave his wife, but he was immediately occupied with navigating his ship and the constant companionship and camaraderie that his men provided. It was good to be out on the seas again and to smell the tang of salt in his nostrils; he had never felt so alive!

The princess, though, felt only despair; she had far less to occupy her mind, and the bridal bed felt cold and empty. She slept poorly; her mind tossed and turned, constantly filled with terrifying thoughts of how her husband might be lost at sea or killed in battle. Her appetite was poor, and she grew pale, wan and restless, unable to settle to any task. Her maids tried to keep her busy, and after some months, the princess seemed to emerge from her lethargy. But there was something gnawing at her mind, an unhappy look upon her lovely features and when questioned, the words tumbled out, 'What if my husband finds another? What if he is unfaithful to me? All men need a woman to warm their sheets!' The princess burst into tears and would not be consoled, no matter how much her women protested and reminded her of Olaf's deep and true love.

After many weeks of torment, the princess woke one morning calm and clear-eyed. Her maids were relieved, but not for long.

'I have a plan,' the princess declared. 'When Prince Olaf returns, if all is well with him and we see the white flag, we will go out to greet him, but I will raise the black flag and lie as if dead in our boat. I will know by his actions whether I am still the love of his life.'

Although her maids tried hard to dissuade the young wife, she was determined that her husband could have been unfaithful, and only by this means would she find out the truth.

Many months had passed by the time Prince Olaf and his men returned, battle weary but triumphant. As the galley entered Loch Maree, he ordered the white sail to be raised high on the mast so that his beautiful wife was sure to see that all was well with him. Eagerly he cried for his men to pull hard on the oars, but the wind was against them and it was a hard haul.

Further down the loch, the lookouts relayed the news that Prince Olaf was returned and that all was well. There was great rejoicing to see the white flag billowing out above the ship.

The maids once again tried to persuade the princess to change her mind, and not go through with her plan, but she remained determined. She dressed as if in her death attire, and was laid out on the boat as if it was her funeral bier. Finally, she ordered the black flag to be raised. Obediently, her servants did as they were bid; distressed that such a joyful day was to be soured by the wife's mistrust.

The galley made its way down the loch, and Olaf's anticipation and excitement grew. He would see his lovely wife soon, and the thought made him delirious with happiness. Every few minutes, he would shout up to the lookout asking if there was any sign of a boat coming in their direction.

When the lookout saw what was approaching, he was reluctant to tell his prince, but he could not withhold the information.

When he heard the news of the black flag, Olaf's face changed; it darkened, his eyes began to blaze and he was overwhelmed with a feeling he didn't know. For the first time in his life he knew fear. He began to shout in panic, and raved at his men to pull faster as he restlessly paced the deck, unable to contain himself.

By the time they reached his wife's boat, Prince Olaf was in a crazed, mad state. He could only see the black flag, a death bier and the form of his beautiful wife beneath a white shroud. He leapt into the boat and knelt down by his princess. Gently, he raised the silken covering. There below lay his lovely lass, white, still, and to his mind, dead. He let out a groan of deep anguished pain and then, with one swift movement, he pulled out his dagger and thrust it deep into his heart. He slumped dead where he knelt, and in the stunned silence that followed, his princess opened her eyes, now convinced of his love for her. But what was her horror to find, not her beloved bent over her in grief, but a dead man, his blood flowing out from his breast; his life gone.

With a wail of remorse and grief, the princess sprang up. She seized the handle of Olaf's dagger, hauled it from her dear husband's breast, and before anyone could stop her, she plunged it into herself. Her own death was agonisingly slow, and she died in torment, knowing her actions had led to this awful tragedy.

Both the prince and princess were mourned deeply by all who knew them. They were buried side by side on Isle Maree, and their ancient graves can still be seen on the island to this day, their story told by many from Kinlochewe to Gairloch.

✧ Wifies or Witches? ✧ – a legend fae Tain

In today's society it seems that many things can be tolerated that previously were regarded as wrong or even evil. In times past, superstition held sway over many lives; fear and ignorance are receptive pupils! Witchcraft was often blamed when there were unusual or catastrophic incidents that could not be explained in any other way. Essie Stewart, a traveller who now lives in Sutherland, told me this tale of witches, which she heard from her grandfather. GB

Many years ago there lived a woman called Mór Bhàn in the village of Drumbeg. Her name means 'Fair Morag', but it is said that she dabbled in the dark arts and it was not good to make mention of Mór Bhàn in Assynt.

From time to time, Mór Bhàn would travel east to Tarbet on the other side of Tain. There she would meet with a woman on the shore at night. She too dabbled in the dark arts and was known as Wee Steinie. They would row away out on the firth, and when they returned, their boat was always teeming with fish, some of which they kept while the rest they would sell.

There was one poor soul of a man that lived in Tain, who was known locally as Reannach, which in Gaelic means mackerel, because this is what he fished for. Now Reannach was curious as to how these two women never ceased to bring home a good catch. One night, he decided to follow them out to sea. It was still and dark, with only the whisper of lapping waves on the sea. Sound can carry very easily over water on a night like that, so Reannach was very careful of his oars, dipping them in and out as quietly as he could, so as not to be noticed.

Eventually the women reached a favoured spot far out from the shore and let down their oars. Sinking their finely woven net, they both began to recite a rhyme. Within minutes, the net began to fill with fish and the women had trouble hauling in their catch. Well pleased with their night's work, the women took up their oars and rowed for shore.

From that time, whenever the women appeared in Tain to go out fishing, Reannach would take his boat and follow the women far out on the firth, and once he had learned the rhyme, he began to use it himself, with good success.

One night, as the women were out at sea, they caught sight of Reannach's boat and heard him reciting their magic. They called out, 'What do you think you are doing here, Reannach?'

The man called back, 'I am fishing … You are fishing!'

'And how did you learn that rhyme?'

'Well, I was listening to you! I learnt your wee rhyme, and it is very good for catching the fish!'

'Go home with you, Reannach, go home now, or it will be the worse for you!'

The man, shaken by their warning, quickly rowed back to shore, but he was stung by their treatment and, feeling angry, he could not keep it to himself. In the inn he blurted out what had happened, and three young lads from the village, all bold heroes, took it upon themselves to deal with the women. They waited on the two crones to return. As time passed, their fear and young bravado stirred them into a rage, so that by the time the women hauled their boat ashore, the three men were out of control. They picked up rocks and stoned Wee Steinie to death. But before the poor woman died, she spoke a curse. She declared that none of the three men would die in their own beds, and not one of them did.

Wee Steinie was regarded as a witch and was not given a Christian burial in the kirkyard. She was buried outside on unhallowed ground in an unmarked grave. But what happened to Mór Bhàn of Drumbeg? To this day, no one knows.

✧ The Second Sight ✧ – legends fae Brahan to Ardguy

When I was on Skye several years ago, I visited the Fairy Glen by Uig. It is a magical green, grassy place with unusual knolls and intriguing rock formations. It struck me how quiet and deserted it was, yet at one time it had been densely populated; over three thousand people lived there. While exploring, I found a circular stone with a hole in the middle. I placed it to my eye, and was inspired to create a story, which seemed to emerge from the mists of time. Recently I was intrigued to discover that in tales of the Brahan Seer, a stone with a hole in its centre, called the seer stone, was often associated with those who had the second sight. GB

✧ A Man of Legend ✧

There are many tales told about the Brahan Seer. The following account is taken from the writings of Alexander Mackenzie and Elizabeth Sutherland, who sought to collect and preserve prophecies attributed to the Brahan Seer.

In the seventeenth century, a child was born at Uig on the Isle of Lewis, named Kenneth Mackenzie, or Coinneach Odhar. When he grew up, Coinneach found work as a farm labourer on the Brahan estate in Easter Ross, which was owned by the Seaforth Mackenzie family.

Coinneach was a perceptive man; he had a quick wit and a confident bearing, and was not afraid to speak his mind to those above his station. His mistress Lady Seaforth took a great dislike to his outspoken manner, and there came a day when she had had enough.

Coinneach was labouring several miles from the house. He had been working hard from sunrise, and was so exhausted that when he sat down, he fell asleep, and was only woken by a maid arriving with his lunch pail. As Coinneach sat up, he felt something pressing on his chest and discovered a small stone, with a hole in its centre, trapped under his jacket. He frowned, feeling the stone's weight in his hand, then, slowly, he lifted it to his left eye and looked through it. Immediately, he was blinded in that one eye, but to his astonishment, he found he had a perception beyond sight; his inner eye had been opened. With sudden clarity, he knew beyond doubt that his mistress had poisoned his food. He deliberately set it before his collie, which wolfed it down eagerly. Coinneach watched, bemused, as his pet writhed in agony until it finally died.

From that day onwards, whenever Coinneach put the stone to his eye, he saw beyond the natural realm, be it in the present or the future. People up and down the land began to seek out the seer; some respected his prophecies, while others ridiculed them.

One gentleman from Inverness requested permission to write down some of Coinneach's prophecies and the seer agreed. Coinneach recounted various prophecies, including one about Inverness. He said, 'One day boats will sail around the back of the Fairy Hill called Tomnahurich.'

The man looked up from his ink and pen.

'Eh man? What did ye say?'

Coinneach repeated his words, and watched the scribe's features turn purple as he spoke, 'What utter nonsense!'

'I tell you,' said the seer, 'one day Tomnahurich will be under lock and key, and the fairies secured within it.'

'That'll nivver happen! Preposterous!' The man was so disgruntled, he threw his still-drying manuscript into the fire.

In 1803, over a century later, the construction of the Caledonian Canal was begun, which skirted Tomnahurich. In the twentieth century a cemetery was built on the hill, surrounded by fences and secured with a lockable gate.

At the beginning of the twentieth century, it was proposed that a new Episcopalian church be built in Strathpeffer. The villagers petitioned that the church be built without a spire. When enquiries were made, it was discovered that locals were terrified of a fifth church being built, as it would fulfil a prediction made by the Brahan Seer.

Mrs Macrae was the most vocal of the petitioners. 'Aye Rector, ye see, auld Coinneach foretold that when there were five spires in the Strath, ships would sail o'er the town and anchor tae the houses!'

Despite the genuine concern expressed by the ardent adherents of the Seer's word, the church was built, spire and all, with no immediate cause for alarm. But, during the First World War, an airship quietly sailed over the rooftops of Strathpeffer and one of the grapnels became entangled in a church spire.

One of the many predictions associated with the Seer was the dreadful slaughter at Culloden: 'Oh Drumossie! Thy bleak moor shall … be stained with the best blood of the Highlands. Glad am I that I will not see the day … heads will be lopped off by the score and no mercy shown or quarter given on either side.'

Following this massacre, and the end of the Jacobite rebellion, the Highland way of life was changed forever. One of the most damaging reforms allowed clan land to be sold to absentee landlords. Such men only wanted to make a profit out of the 'acres of empty land' through sheep farming. Families were forced off the land where they had lived and worked for generations, and the Seer's prophecy was remembered: 'Sheep shall eat men, men will eat sheep.'

Coinneach himself, however, was not to live to a ripe old age, for his honesty was to bring him to a bitter end. While Lord Seaforth was in Paris, his wife asked the seer for an account of her husband's behaviour, and Coinneach dutifully told her of Seaforth's infidelity. Coinneach's answer angered and humiliated Lady Seaforth, and she ordered his immediate death. Coinneach was tarred and burned alive in a barrel at the Chanonry of Ross. The seer's final curse over the Seaforth family was of an end to the Clan Mackenzie, with various signs unfolding as proof of the prophecy, which came to pass before the century was through.

Coinneach Odhar held much sway over the nation with the words from his mouth. In certain circles, his memory is still spoken of with reverence and his second-sight predictions believed without doubt.

✧ A Man of Fact ✧

I have wondered at the Brahan Seer's ability to accurately predict the future. Unless his words were scribed as he spoke them, how could it be proved that he was indeed the author of these predictions? For those who have written of the Brahan Seer's prophecies, where did they hear them? From where or whom did their sources hear them? It is fascinating.

I myself do not doubt the gift of second sight; I have seen it in various forms over the years, but can this one man be the source of so many prophecies? The legends around him seem fallible and romanticised and the predictions often appear to be made to fit many modern-day happenings.

In his book The Brahan Seer: The Making of a Legend, *Alex Sutherland begins to unravel some of the mystery surrounding Coinneach Odhar. He examines the way in which we believe information about the past. For example, he highlights how once the spoken word is written, it can then be regarded by some as the defining truth on a topic; in this case, the Brahan Seer and his prophecies. Sutherland's thorough examination of this topic makes fascinating reading and the following summary is taken from Alex's book with his kind permission.*

Historically, there are no records of this man's existence in the seventeenth century, but 100 years earlier a Keanoch Owir is mentioned. His name is associated with the witches who were prevalent in the area at the time, and he was regarded as a leader and principal 'enchantress' amongst them. Lady Fowlis, the second wife of Robert Munro of Easter Ross, was attempting to secure her future by eliminating her stepson and his wife, and she sought the witches' assistance. When this scheme proved unsuccessful, she resorted to poison, but this mistakenly caused the death of her servant. Lady Fowlis was brought to trial, and as a result, it was highlighted how powerful the local coven of witches had become in their influence.

All over Scotland towards the latter end of the sixteenth century, there was an increasing drive to cleanse the land of witchcraft. Even King James VI had become increasingly concerned about the control that witches exerted, after his own life came under threat in 1590. After this instance, he exhorted a round-up of those guilty of witchcraft to be tried and sentenced according to their guilt.

In 1577, following Lady Fowlis' trial, a Royal Commission was formed from Holyroodhouse, giving permission to hunt and bring to trial those accused of witchcraft. This resulted in the sentencing of nine witches, who were burned to death at the Chanonry of Ross. Although the commission named Keanoch Owir as culpable, he eluded justice. A second Royal Commission was issued in 1578, and this categorically named Keanoch Owir as the leader of witchery and devilish deeds.

Was this Coinneach Odhar? Other records from this period reveal that in 1576, the wife of the Provost of Inverness had a manservant known as Kennocht Owyr, whom she accused of shady dealings. Her servant traded in skins, which may have been marketed at several fairs in the area. If this were the witch Coinneach Odhar, it would make the perfect alibi for appearing at fairs. A coven of witches might gather without suspicion amongst crowds of people coming to market.

Sutherland explains that by the seventeenth century, the Seaforth Mackenzies had superseded the Munros of Fowlis as the most influential family in Easter Ross. At this time, there were still witch-hunts taking place, but by then, although gentry might accuse individuals and bring them to judgement, the meting out of justice would have been in the hands of the church and state. As such, it is unlikely, as the story suggests, that Lady Seaforth was able to take Coinneach Odhar's execution into her own hands.

There are a number of similarities between the Coinneach Odhar legends of the seventeenth century and those pertaining to Kennocht Owyr of the sixteenth century. Were the two one and the same? Is this the man that many regard as the Brahan Seer?

✧ A Genuine Man ✧

One day I was in the car with a work colleague, Robert. I was telling him about some of the stories I had been researching, including the Brahan Seer. 'Oh,' says he, 'my dad knew the Brahan Seer!' I said, 'That could be a bit tricky as he lived a few centuries ago!' 'No, no, no,' said Robert, 'my father knew the Seer …' and he proceeded to tell me a little about Swene Macdonald, who was well known in the Highlands for his foretellings. I realised this was a man who might be worth hearing more about and Robert Aitken (senior) kindly agreed to speak with me. Robert had first met the Seer when he heard that Swene was in possession of some very old weapons, which he wanted to sell. Robert was an antiques dealer and was interested in buying them. Swene was pleased; he now had the money to get his jeep back on the road! This was the beginning of a mutual friendship, which continued over the years and was valued by both men. GB

Swene Macdonald was a genuine man who would never try to hoodwink you. His fair hair was turning grey and was long to his collar; his beard was greyish black. But the thing that struck you about the man was his eyes; he had piercing blue eyes that looked right through you.

He lived on a croft, a mile outside of Ardguy and worked the land for as long as he was able.

As a young man Swene had found he could foretell certain things and as time passed, local people began to come to his door for help. His reputation grew and men and women would come to visit the Seer from all over the country and further afield, including the United States.

For as long as he lived Swene Macdonald was honourable in what he did; he never asked for payment. When asked how much he charged Swene would say, 'It is up to yourself what you give me; as long as I have enough to live on.' Swene would not betray anyone's confidence and he turned no one away. Whether you were a tramp or a millionaire, it made no difference, he would treat you just the same, he was there to help. In his gentle Highland lilt he would say, 'Come in me lassie, sit down and don't worry about a thing.'

His fame grew and celebrities began to visit. Swene agreed to be interviewed on a chat show called *Pebblemill at One*, all expenses paid. This was a great success; people were amazed at his gift and the Seer was in all the papers.

He foretold that the Dornoch Bridge would collapse in the future and the locals are sure that in time this will happen.

One American woman was told she had a long-lost brother on the other side of the world and when she investigated the records, she discovered that she did indeed have a brother who for some reason had been adopted. She managed to trace him to Australia and since then they have been reunited.

As Swene became older, he began to look worn out and tired. He turned more and more to drink, perhaps to relieve himself of the burdens he carried. One day he confided in Robert saying, 'I've so much on my mind.'

Swene Macdonald died in 2010, a well-respected man, better known as the Grand Seer of the Highlands.

✧ The Old Woman by the Clootie Well ✧ – a legend fae the Black Isle

Munlochy village lies in the heart of the Black Isle, close to a wooded area that houses a collection of famous clootie trees. Such trees were common once throughout Scotland and Ireland, usually situated by holy wells reputed to have healing qualities. An Act of Parliament in Scotland banned making a pilgrimage to a holy well in 1581. The Holy Well at Munlochy pre-dates the time of St Boniface/Curitan, who worked as a missionary in the area in AD *620. SB*

Pagans would visit the well and walk around it three times following the direction of the sun. Then they would tie a cloot, which is a piece of cloth, to a branch of the nearest tree. When the rag rotted away, so did the ailment. When the cloth faded, the belief was that it carried wishes out into the elements and away forever. It continues to be visited, particularly on the old Celtic festival of Beltane on 1 May.

✧ Wolves o' Scotland ✧

It was when visiting the Clootie Well at Munlochy that I met an old woman of the road selling bits of lucky heather to passing visitors. Feeling sorry for her, I gave her a pound for a sprig, though I knew full well that I could have filled a bin with heather just up the road for free. I was stepping away from her when two teenage girls ran up, circling the old woman and making wolf-howling noises, mocking and tormenting her. To my shame, I did not intervene, but the girls soon tired of the sport and ran off. I stepped up to apologise and offer any help, but the old woman shrugged and sat down on a boulder by the roadside. 'What do they know about wolves, those trash of girls?' she asked. And right there under the clootie tree, she began to tell me facts and tales about the wolves of Scotland. SB

Long ago wolves were once so common in Scotland that Sutherland folk buried their dead off the coast on the small sea-stack of Handa, to prevent the wolves from disinterring and eating them. In the reign of James VI spittals or shelters were built on isolated roads for the safety of travellers at night, who might come under wolf attack.

'On Ederachillis' Shore' by Eliza Ann Harris, *A Book of Highland Minstrelsy* (1846)

On Ederachillis' shore
The grey wolf lies in wait-
Woe to the broken door,
Woe to the loosened gate,
And the groping wretch whom sleety fogs
On the trackless moor be late.

The lean and hungry wolf,
With his fangs so sharp and white,
His starveling body pinched
By the frost of a northern night,
And his pitiless eyes that scare the dark
With their green and threatening light.

He climbs the guarding dyke,
He leaps the hurdle bars,
He steals the sheep from the pen,
And the fish from the boat-house spars,
And he digs the dead from out of the sod,
And gnaws them under the stars.

Thus every grave we dug
The hungry wolf up tore,
And every morn the sod
Was strewn with bones and gore:
Our mother-earth had denied us rest
On Ederchallis' shore.

The custom of island burial was also used on Tanera Mor and on Inishail. In Atholl, five flagstones were used to wolf-proof coffins. In 1527 James I ordered his subjects to carry out three wolf-hunts per year between the months of April and August when wolves give birth to their cubs. In 1563 Mary Queen of Scots hunted wolves in the great woodlands of Atholl, with 2,000 highlanders. They killed five wolves on that occasion.

When Was the Last Wolf Killed?

Killiecrankie

Officially, it was recorded that Sir Ewan Cameron claimed the honour in 1680 in Perthshire.

Glen Moriston

Another 'last wolf' was supposedly killed in Glen Moriston by a woman. She was on her way home from taking food to her kinsfolk who were out cutting peat, when she was confronted by a wolf. Thinking fast she wrapped a towel around her hand, and using her knife, she rammed this into the wolf's open jaws, thus saving her own life and relieving the wolf of his.

Brora

On the A9 close to Brora is a stone, marking where the last wolf was killed by a hunter called Polson who came from Wester Helmsdale in 1700.

Polson and his two lads had tracked a wolf to its lair in Glen Loth, while the mother was away. The boys managed to squeeze into the den to kill the wolf cubs. Suddenly the mother appeared and raced past Polson and squeezed into the den to rescue her young. Polson caught her by the tail and pulled her back, but her head was blocking the entrance.

'Father, what is keeping the light from us?' one son cried in Gaelic.

'If the root of the tail breaks you'll soon know that,' Polson replied, but after a struggle he killed the mother with his dirk.

Cawdor

In the annals of Scottish folklore, McQueen of Findhorn in Morayshire slew the last wolf in 1743 in Tarnaway Forest.

McQueen had received a message from the Chief of Clan Mackintosh that a while a mother had been travelling over the hills from Cawdor with her two children a wolf had slain both boys. A Tinchel or a hunters' gathering was called together, but there was no sign of McQueen. When he did appear, he was upbraided for being so late. In response he drew the head of the wolf from under his plaid and flung it down on the ground. He said, 'As I came through the ravine by east the hill there, I foregathered wi the beast. My hound turned him. I bucked wi him, an dirkit (stabbed) him, syne cut his throat and brought awa his countenance for fear he might come alive again, for they are very precarious creatures.'

Sutherland

Renowned storyteller Bob Pegg was given an original article written in The Northern Times *from 26 September 1929, which he tells in his book* Highland Folk Tales. *This account was given by the guest of a shooting tenant and concerned a wolf sighting in Sutherland in 1888. The hunter had lost his way in thick mist and finding himself in a cave in the glen of Dionard, he set a small fire and went to sleep and waited for morning.*

I awoke with a great start and looked at my watch. It was one o'clock in the morning, and the weather had cleared. The moon appeared and the stars shone with a flickering and a frosty lustre like great diamonds on the black corsage of night. A musty odour had become most intense, and as my sleepy eyes threw off their shattered torpor, I saw with a shiver of apprehension a pair of sunken baleful looking eyes regarding me steadily and stealthily across the dying embers of the fire.

I slipped a couple of cartridges into my gun, and as I did so I heard a low painful whine. I could now make out a white form like a huge dog lying not more than three feet from me. Its head rested on its paws and so far from showing any signs of hostility, it seemed to exhibit symptoms of friendliness. Its coat was a kind of silver-grey in colour and was thick and curly, but the face showed signs of great age.

I stood up with my gun at my shoulder, but the beast did not move, and I could not find it in my heart to shoot; instead I threw it a ham sandwich. It nosed it wearily, but did not attempt to eat it, so I offered it a cheese one, which it rejected with some evidence of repulsion. The creature then rose, and I saw to my unbounded astonishment that a great silver-grey female wolf faced me. She whined again, but kept her distance, and I then saw that in her eyes brooded a look of unutterable loneliness and misery.

A female wolf, and the last wolf had been killed in Sutherland between 1690 and 1700. I could have gained lasting glory by shooting her, but my hand was stayed. It was I who had invaded her poor little dwelling, and she had shared it with me without hostility. She should suffer no harm from me. Her ancestors had wandered here when Scotland was joined to Greenland, and had shared these wan wastes with the majestic elk and the ivory-tusked boar; fighting and suffering and dying in those vast oak and pine forests, the remains of which are still visible in the great mosses which abound all over Sutherland.

A MIX O' URBAN TALE SHORTIES

In this part of the book, let Sheena entertain you with urban myths of gore, fun, horror and taste.

✧ Glasgow Shorties ✧

Let the Fun Continue

The council had planned to install a plinth at a cost of £65,000 to raise the height of the Duke of Wellington's statue, which stands outside the Gallery of Modern Art on Queen Street. This was an attempt to deter revellers from depositing a traffic cone on the top of Wellington's head. This civic plan would have ended a fond Glaswegian tradition; but thankfully, on 12 November 2013, it was abandoned due to the furious outrage of the public and backlash from the media.

Elvis Connection

Who can forget that Glasgow was the only place Elvis visited in Britain? He passed through the fair city in 1960 while returning from army service in Germany.

Kelvingrove Rumours

Everywhere you turn in Glasgow, myths sprout up like mushrooms. Glasgow's Kelvingrove Museum opened in 1901 and there are two myths associated with it. SB

The building was apparently erected the wrong way round.

The architect was so upset by his 'mistake' that he committed suicide by jumping off one of its towers.

Unidentified

Glasgow has had recent contact with an Unidentified Flying Object, a UFO. A passenger plane was reported by the UK Airprox Board as having had a 'near-miss'. SB

A startled pilot of an Airbus A320 alerted traffic controllers to the presence of 'something' passing just 400 feet under his plane as it was approaching Glasgow Airport on 2 December 2012. It was a clear day and the plane was flying at 4,000 feet above Glasgow, preparing to descend. The landing lights were on when the crew suddenly saw a UFO speed below them. It was moving fast; observers described it as yellow or silver and bigger than a balloon. But, interestingly, air traffic control said nothing had appeared on radar. Twenty-eight seconds earlier at Prestwick, traffic control had picked up something flying a mile and a half east of the plane, but no one could identify it.

Nasty Taste

Whilst I was enjoying a city tour around Glasgow, I was seated just behind a couple chatting about a foiled theft on the outskirts of the town. Intrigued, I listened to the following account. SB

John and May O'Hare were from Glasgow and had been touring around Scotland in their camper van. On their last night they were close to home, but were too tired to go the whole way, so they had parked their camper beside the road in a layby. While they were asleep, a thief appeared with a plastic hose and fuel container, hoping to poach some diesel from their van. He stuck one end of the hose in his mouth to get the siphon going and in the darkness he stuck the other end into what he thought was the fuel reserves, but he mistook the septic tank for the fuel tank. In the morning, O'Hare stepped outside the van to find the plastic hose lying on the ground and beside it was the fuel container, the entire contents of the septic tank and a puddle of human vomit.

Not the Nicest Smile

In the early 1990s rumours were rife amongst the children of Glasgow that gangs of men dressed up in clown costumes were roaming the streets in royal blue transit vans. SB

It was believed that some escaped psychopaths from Carstairs Asylum were on the lookout for children, with the intention of maiming and disfiguring them. It was said that on capturing one, they would give the child 'a Glasgow smile' by slashing the boy or girl's mouth from ear to ear. There are many reported sightings, but no concrete evidence. This however did not deter some yobs from egging a blue van belonging to an innocent couple.

✧ Edinburgh Shorties ✧

Touring the City

Most travellers visit the capital city of Edinburgh. A good way to see around the city is to find a guided tour. Let me take you on a short one now. SB

With Evil Intent

Many of Edinburgh's tour guides are dressed in costume and this one night, one was dressed as a highwayman, and was taking a party of tourists round the Old Town. SB

The guide was regaling his group with tales of riotous times in the past, when a man burst out from a narrow thoroughfare brandishing a machete. At first, the group thought that this character was laid on for their entertainment. But in fact this man had suffered beyond endurance from the repetitive supernatural tours below his flat every night. He could no longer cope with howling, screaming, reacting tourists!

It was only when this crazed man began to chase the party of tourists that they realised his intention was to kill, not thrill.

Door Decor

The tale of the drunk at the door is one with which you may be familiar. SB

In 1825 a lady called Mrs Campbell stayed in an old town house in Edinburgh. One night a thunderous knocking on the door woke her from her sleep; by the noise she deduced it was a party of drunken revellers. Wisely, she stayed in bed. Next morning, she went downstairs and opened the door. She examined the knocker and found that the brass had been torn and twisted alarmingly. Not only that, but part of the vandal's finger had been wrenched off, and remained ominously embedded in what remained of the metal.

The World's End

Any self-respecting tour guide will definitely steer you in the direction of Mary King's Close, taking you back to a scene from 1645, during the plague days. SB

Those afflicted by the plague had to hang white sheets from their windows, to be seen by a plague doctor. John Paulitious was the first doctor, who died quickly, in June 1645. The second doctor was George Rae, who dressed himself in a large beaked mask stuffed with sweet herbs, and a full-length leather coat and cape, with leather boots and gloves. Rae would lance open the buboes of his patients and sterilize them with a red-hot poker. Many died of shock. It is little wonder that a nearby close goes by the name of 'The World's End'.

To attempt to contain the disease, one area around Mary King's Close was sealed off, with its occupants inside it. The sufferings endured by those miserable victims must have been indescribable. Today, it has become a major tourist attraction in Edinburgh. Visitors enter the close through Warriston's Close and Writers' Court. A little before the close was turned into a major attraction, a famous Japanese psychic is said to have visited. There, she became aware of a spirit called Annie, who had been a little plague victim, and was very distressed to have lost her doll. The psychic stepped into the sunshine of the High Street from the gloom and dankness of the ancient musty close, and bought a doll and placed it in Annie's room. The spirit seemed to find comfort in that. Now, from all over the world, people bring dolls and toys to that room, as well as money donations. The money is regularly collected and handed over to the Sick Children's Friends Foundation. More than £40,000 has already been donated.

Haunted House

An enterprising guide will make a detour to William Brien House. A strange happening occurred in one of the rooms of this house in Inverleith; it gained a forbidding reputation as being haunted. SB

A medical student called Andrew Muir approached the owners of William Brien's house and asked to spend a night there for a dare. He was given a bell to summon them if he got into any difficulties.

In the early hours of the morning, the owners heard the bell ring furiously and loud screams emanated from the haunted room. When they rushed in, they were too late. Andrew was dead, bleeding from puncture wounds to his shoulder and his neck.

The murder was never solved, though many named the previous owner, William Brien, as a supernatural suspect. Brien had been a recluse and on his deathbed he had given strict instructions that his coffin was to be firmly secured and he was to be buried 40 feet deep in the ground.

Heart of Midlothian

In the middle of Edinburgh there is a heart-shaped mosaic in the street close to the west door of St Giles High Kirk, known as The Heart of Midlothian. SB

The heart marks the spot of what was once the middle of a condemned cell in the Tolbooth, which was demolished in 1817. On the way to be hanged the doomed man would spit on the cell floor to show his contempt for the law.

✧ Meal and Ale Scottish Style ✧

While in Scotland, it is imperative to sample some of our culinary delights. Let me highlight some of them for you. SB

The Haggis

For the true seeker of gastronomic delights, a traveller could do no better than sample the cuisine of Scotland. Forget your Kopi Luwak coffee beans harvested from the poo of the civet, a Vietnamese delicacy at £50 per kilo. Cease to hanker for the bird-spit soup of Hong Kong or the Indonesian 'piece de resistance' of live monkey brain. Even the Korean dish of live baby octopus (chew the tentacles carefully, in case they attempt to strangle you on the way down) pale by comparison with the Scottish haggis. SB

Few foods have a day to themselves on the calendar. But on 25 January, which is referred to as Burns' Night, Scots worldwide recite a long ode to the creation of the haggis, before slitting it open with brio and panache. The haggis itself is a concoction of lambs' livers, hearts, lungs and trimmings, mixed with oatmeal and diced onions, spiced and stuffed into a sheep's stomach.

Generally it is a man who undertakes the gralloching of the haggis but I was once invited to perform the function by the folk of the village of Dunecht. The previous year, the man addressing the haggis was so carried away by the occasion that he brought the dagger down too hard, and smashed the plate it rested upon. That particular year the assembled company had to feast on tatties, better known as potatoes, neeps or turnips and spam, which is tinned processed meat.

Prior to feasting on haggis, a custom has also grown up of 'haggis hurling'. At the Milngavie Highland Games on 11 June 2011, Lorne Coltart made a world record throw of 217 feet. The only rule for this competition is that the haggis must not split on landing, so it can be eaten with impunity afterwards.

Atholl Brose

A gastronome should also enjoy sampling Atholl Brose. SB

Legend has it that the Earl of Atholl invented Atholl Brose to win a clan war in 1475. He filled a well with the drink made from honey, oatmeal and whisky and the opposing clan, on drinking it, became too drunk to carry out any pillaging or raping.

Heather Ale

Perhaps heather ale would be more to the gourmet's liking? As with most things Scottish, it comes with attendant legend. SB

There was once a tribe of folk in Scotland called the Pechs. They were all small and red haired with long arms and huge feet but their most important asset was their knowledge of the recipe to brew heather ale. Upon his deathbed each Pech father would hand down the secret recipe to his son. For hundreds of years the Pechs habitually fought amongst each other with vendettas and feuds, but there came a sad time when there were only two Pechs left alive, an old father and his son.

Now the King of Scotland loved his heather ale, and was determined to find out the recipe before it was too late. The last two Pechs were captured and taken before him; they were ordered to disclose the secret recipe on pain of torture. The old man took the king aside.

'Ye maun kill my son, afore I tell you how we brew the ale frae the heather bell.'

The king thought this a queer request, but he had the young Pech beheaded. Then the old Pech laughed in the king's face.

'My son was a weak laddie. He'd hae telt ye under torture. Bit I'll nae tell ye!'

Deep Fried Mars Bar

No self-respecting epicure can visit Scotland without tasting a deep fried Mars Bar. A survey discovered that more than a fifth of Scots chip shops were serving this calorie-packed food. Dr Morrison from the NHS Greater Glasgow Health Board conducted the study. Children, it seemed, love them. Dr Morrison was quoted as saying, 'We can now confirm that there is no doubt, the deep fried Mars Bar is not just an urban myth.' SB

This delicacy was first produced in 1995 in the Haven Chip Bar in Stonehaven. The Aberdeen Evening Express was the first newspaper to alert the world and on 24 August 1995, the *Daily Herald* published the article 'Mars Supper Please'. The news of this odd companion with chips then went out on the BBC World news.

Porridge

Possibly you have seen early TV adverts of a muscular, kilted Scot, standing on a ladder to retrieve the other national food, porridge oats. A PhD could be written on porridge and the Scottish psyche. SB

For those with a competitive streak, you could do worse than travel to the Highland village of Carrbridge every October, to take part in the World Porridge-Making Championships, to try to win the prize of the golden spurtle. One prize-winning team took the competition so seriously, they took a pre-porridge-stirring dip in the freezing waters of the North Sea off Lossiemouth.

Competitors in the past have ranged from an English chef trained at Le Gavroche in London, and an Israeli who produced smoked-fish porridge, entering under the 'speciality' category of porridge.

Dr Johnson's statement that oats were 'a grain, which in England is generally given to horses, but in Scotland appears to support the people', shows how little he knew of the benefits of a hearty plate of porridge. Rumour has it that it aids the libido and it certainly reduces the danger of contracting diabetes. Some claim that it cures hangovers. In the days before antiseptic, a porridge poultice was used to suck out pus. It reduces obesity, perks up the immune system, counteracts depression and high blood-pressure and is, of course, cheap! However, never stir your porridge to the left unless you want to raise the Devil.

The folk of St Kilda, apparently, liked to boil a puffin in their porridge, as a substitute for salt, having removed the beak and feathers first.

All over Scotland at one time it was common for families to cook a weekly batch of porridge and pour it into a kitchen drawer. From there, it was served by the slice, when cold.

But let us not forget the impoverished student from Aberdeen who was reported to have been the last case of scurvy in Britain. His sole source of food was porridge; you can have too much of a good thing. At the end of his third year he was admitted to hospital as Aberdeen's first recorded case of scurvy in 120 years.

The more sales-savvy amongst us have explored new avenues for porridge. The first porridge bar in the world was called 'Stoats' in Edinburgh; it was established by three Edinburgh graduates, in a retro American 1960s van. They served organic porridge, whisky and honey porridge, white chocolate and roasted hazelnut porridge, and even cranachan porridge, which is porridge with clotted cream and raspberries.

Irn Bru

If you require something to wash down your porridge, it is absolutely imperative that you try the Scottish national drink of Irn Bru.

Every Scotsman knows about the orange, fizzy soft drink packed with iron. 'Brewed in Scotland from Girders' was the 1970s slogan for Irn Bru. Scotland's greatest athlete, Donald Dinnie, was the first man to be featured advertising this marvellous beverage. He competed in sixteen highland games seasons in Scotland, and also toured the United States' Caledonian Circuit in 1870. SB

The chairman of Irn Bru was one of only two people in the world to know the recipe, and the two 'in the know' never travelled on the same plane.

Once every month the components for the drink were personally mixed in the secrecy of a sealed room at the company's former headquarters in Cumbernauld. Thirty-two different ingredients bubbled away in a huge vat, which mixed 8,000 litres at a time. The recipe was discovered in 1901 and has not changed in 108 years. Apparently the secret formula has been written down for posterity and is stored in a bank vault in Scotland.

Every hard-drinking Scot will tell you that Irn Bru is a sure-fire cure for a hangover. Some have even credited the higher percentage of ginger-haired babies in Scotland to be a direct result of mothers drinking it during pregnancy. Its fame and popularity has even penetrated the Kremlin. There is an advert showing pregnant Kremlin guards with a voiceover stating, 'It's not six months. It's six bottles of Irn Bru!'

There is also reputed to be an advert of a cow which announces, 'When I'm a burger, I want to be washed down with Irn Bru.'

One of the oddest adverts in the Irn Bru publicity campaign displayed babies suckling breasts with the thought bubble, 'Ooh, good. Mum's been on the Irn Bru again.'

In the Museum of Scotland, it is said there are a range of exhibits on display chosen by Scottish celebrities. Sean Connery's choice was a crate of Irn Bru!

Spit tae Thicken

My father was manager of a Highland bus company, which occasionally took bus-loads of tourists on tours of the Aberdeenshire Highlands. During the tour, the bus would stop at a hotel for a midday meal. On these occasions the driver was generally served a free meal in the kitchen with the cooking staff. The tourists were served in the dining room. SB

While eating lunch at the hotel, one American gentleman sent his custard back halfway through dessert, complaining that it was too thin, and demanding that the cook rectify this.

'We canna hae that,' said the chef. Lifting the bowl to his mouth, he spat copiously into it, before handing it back to the waiter to re-serve. 'That'll thicken it up for him. We aim tae please oor customers.'

The driver asked the tourist if he enjoyed the custard.

'Hell yeah,' the man replied. 'It pays to keep those chef guys on their toes.'

Cow Dung Flavour

When my father and his brothers were youngsters, my grandfather, who was a haulage contractor, sent them to load up a cart with cow dung, or sharn, as it is called in Scots. SB

There was always a great demand for one particular farmer's sharn, as he only cleaned out his byre once a year. By that time the poor cows were standing on such a huge pile of straw and dung, they were almost touching the byre roof. As the boys forked the sharn onto the cart, the farmer's wife came out. It was a blistering hot day, and my father had forgotten to take a stoppered bottle of milk with him.

'Never mind, laddie,' said the farmer's wife, 'I'll pour ye oot a drink o' milk frae my coo.'

She then took a jug and milked her cow without washing its teats. A dollop of dung fell into the jug. Seeing my father's look of horror, she remarked, 'Lord sakes, it's only a wee bit sharn. Did ye no ken it's sharn that gies the milk its flavour?'

✧ Other Shorties ✧

Piddlin Matters

There is an urban myth that if a stranger knocks on your door in Scotland requesting to use the toilet, you are legally bound to let them. SB

In 2008 this was voted the fifth most ridiculous law in the country. However, a spokesman for the justice department in Scotland has been quoted as saying that these so-called laws on urination are 'all urban myths as far as we can ascertain'.

One of the members of the UK Law Commission's Statute Law Repeals Team, John Saunders stated that these laws are 'likely to be urban myths. As far as we are aware, they are not part of our statute law and probably never have been. Although we should not rule out the possibility that one or two of them may have been local bye-laws or customs.'

Act of God

Throughout the world the tale of 'the falling cow' is held up as an urban myth. But in my case, it happens to be true. A few years ago, a nephew who had come into possession of a new car invited me out for a spin. Not sure of his driving abilities, I settled for a run out to Skene, in sight of the Hill o' Fare. SB

My nephew drove along a narrow rural road without mishap until confronted by a young boy herding some cattle. My nephew dutifully switched off the ignition, to allow the herd to pass. One particularly dozy creature decided to mount the steep grassy bank on our left, to get around the vehicle. In horror, we watched as the animal lost its balance in slow motion and toppled sideways, falling with an almighty thump onto the bonnet of the car. Needless to say, the car was a write-off. On confronting the farmer, we were greeted with the response, 'Ah well, the insurance doesn't pay out for an act of God!'

The Scottish Kilt

A certain Scot was very drunk when he set off to visit his fiancée. Unfortunately as he left, the fringe of his kilt was trapped in the door. His mother had been weaving tartan for it, and had another 8 yards spare. Arriving at his beloved's house, he flung stones at her window to gain her attention. Once she was looking down at him, he tossed aside his cloak, asking if she liked what she saw, unaware that by now he was totally nude. When she answered in the affirmative, he replied, 'Aye, and I've anither eight yards at hame!'

Tartan on the Moon

Alan LaVern Bean was selected by NASA in 1963 to become an astronaut. His first spaceflight was aboard Apollo 12. SB

Bean was born in Wheeler, Northeast Texas, of Scots descent, and was very proud of his Scots heritage. In 1969 he became the fourth man to walk on the moon. The Scottish Tartans' Authority were 'over the moon' to receive a note from this astronaut along with a piece of tartan, stating:

> To the Scottish Tartans' Authority.
>
> This piece of Macbean tartan was flown to the moon in our Apollo 12 Command Module 'Yankee Clipper'. It was then transferred to our lunar module 'Intrepid' and was placed on the moon in November 1969. I am entrusting this valuable piece of tartan history to your care.
>
> Signed, Alan Bean, Lunar Module Pilot.

Tartan on Mount Everest

A tartan flag was left on top of Mount Everest by Canadian Doug Maclaren. He placed it there in 2001, in honour of his cousin Marnie McBean. He said at the time, 'Just where the name belongs, on top of the world.'

BIBLIOGRAPHY

Sheena Blackhall:

Aberdeen

Keith, Alexander, *A Thousand Years of Aberdeen* (Aberdeen University Press, 1987).

The White Dove Inn and The Hindoo Ghost

O'Donnell, Elliott, *Scottish Ghost Stories* (The Floating Press, 2011), Case XVI.

The Tusk

en.wikipedia.org/wiki/Sigurd_Eysteinsson

The Horseman's Word

Fernee, Ben et al., *The Society of the Horseman's Word* (The Society of Esoteric Endeavour, 2009).

Henderson, Hamish, 'A Slight Case of Devil Worship', *New Statesman and Nation* (1962).

The Wicked and the Tragic

www.smithsonianmag.com/history/the-monster-of-glamis-92015626/

Chess and Hitchhikers

Brunvand, Jan Harold, *The Encyclopedia of Urban Legends*, Updated and Expanded Edition (ABC-CLIO, 2012), under 'Scotland'.

House to Let

Westwood, Jennifer and Sophia Kingshill, *The Lore of Scotland: A Guide to Scottish Legends* (Random House, 2009).

Cannibals on the Royal Mile

Nicholson, John, *Historical and Traditional Tales Connected with the South of Scotland* (1843).

Nine o' Diamonds

'Is the Curse of Scotland in the cards?', *The Scotsman*, 9 March 2006.

The Ballad o' Binnorie

'Binnorie or the Twa Sisters', No 10 in Francis J. Child's *The English and Scottish Popular Ballads* (1882–98).

The Golden Screw

www.iusedtobelieve.com, children's myths and bellybuttons.

A Well Kent Dug

Bondeson, Jan, *Greyfriars Bobby: The Most Faithful Dog in the World* (Amberley Publishing, 2011).

'A very Victorian hoax! Greyfriars Bobby who kept vigil over his master's grave for fourteen years was "a publicity stunt"', *Daily Mail*, 4 August 2011.

Jekyll and Hyde

www.sawneybean.com/horrors/DeaconBrodie.htm

A Close Shave

forum.landrovernet.com/showthread.php/11171-Close-shave-or-what

The Ballad o' Tam Lin

Stewart, A.M. (ed.), *The Complaynt of Scotland* (Scottish Text Society, 1979).

Child, Francis James, *The English and Scottish Popular Ballads* (1882–98).

Wilson, Barbara Ker, *Scottish Folk-Tales and Legends* (Oxford University Press, 1954).

Glasgow

www.glasgow.gov.uk/index.aspx?articleid=2998

The Glasgow Vampire

Nicolson, S., 'Child Vampire Hunters Sparked Comic Crackdown', BBC News Scotland, 22 March 2010. news.bbc.co.uk/1/hi/scotland/8574484.stm

The Gorbals Vampire, BBC Radio 4, 30 March 2010.

Kingston Bridge

'Concrete Tomb: Repairs May Unearth Bodies of Gangsters', *Daily Record*, 2 November 1999. www.thefreelibrary.com

The Rocking Chair

en.wikipedia.org/wiki/The_Devil's_Chair_(urban_legend)

Overtoun Dogs

www.atlasobscura.com/places/overtoun-bridge

'Why Have So Many Dogs Leapt to Their Deaths from Overtoun Bridge?', *Daily Mail*, 17 October 2006.

Robberson, T., 'Bridge Draws Dogs to Jump', *Aiken Standard*, 7 August 2005.

Dunning, Brian, 'The Suicide Dogs of Overton Bridge', Skeptoid Podcast, Episode 320, 24 July 2012. skeptoid.com/episodes/4320

The Little Buddy Hoax, Paisley

Wenner, Cheryl and Alice Lesoravage, 'Myth Produces Mountain Of Mail For "Dying Boy"', *The Morning Call*, 11 March 1987.

A Dragonish Tale

www.forestry.gov.uk

Changelings

Gregor, Walter, *The Folk-Lore of the North-East of Scotland* (The Folk-lore Society, 1881).

www.pitt.edu/~dash/britchange.html

The Mystery of Flannan Isle and the Cormorants

www.bbc.co.uk/dna/place-london/plain/A1061335

A Cave of Dark Deeds

www.smoocave.org

Wulvers

Bane, Theresa, *Encyclopedia of Fairies in World Folklore and Mythology* (McFarland & Co., 2013).

The Clootie Well

www.undiscoveredscotland.co.uk/munlochy/clootiewell/

Wolves o' Scotland

lastwolf.net

Shorties:

Let the Fun Continue

www.bbc.co.uk/news/uk-scotland-glasgow-west-24907190

Elvis in Glasgow

news.bbc.co.uk/1/hi/scotland/glasgow_and_west/7361164.stm

Kelvingrove Rumours

www.glasgowlife.org.uk/museums/kelvingrove/about/Pages/History.aspx

Unidentified

Devlin, Kate, 'Scottish UFO Sightings Rocket', *The Herald*, 21 June 2013.

Nasty Taste

www.foxnews.com/story/2004/05/21/this-doesnt-taste-like-diesel-fuel/

Not the Nicest Smile

fear-theatre.blogspot.co.uk/2011/06/glasgows-killer-clowns-from-carstairs.html

Door Décor

Hobbs, Sandy, 'The Folk Tale as News', *Oral History*, Vol.6, No.2 (Autumn 1978), pp.74–86.

The World's End

www.realmarykingsclose.com

Haunted House

hubpages.com/hub/Scottish-Vampires

The Heart of Midlothian

www.edinburghnotes.com/places/heart-of-midlothian.html

Atholl Brose

Simon, André, *A Concise Encyclopædia of Gastronomy*, Section VIII, Wines and Spirits (The Wine and Food Society, 1948).

Heather Ale: Pechs

Chambers, Robert, *Popular Rhymes of Scotland* (W. & R. Chambers, 1870), pp.80–82.

Deep Fried Mars Bars

'Deep-Fried Mars Myth Is Dispelled', BBC News Scotland, 17 December 2004. news.bbc.co.uk/1/hi/scotland/4103415.stm

'Mars Supper Please', *Daily Herald*, 24 August 1995.

Porridge

Boswell, James. *The Life of Samuel Johnson, LL.D.: Including a Journal of His Tour to the Hebrides*, Volume 3 (Derby & Jackson, 1858), p.11.

World Porridge-Making Championships

www.goldenspurtle.com/

Aberdeen University Review. www.archive.org/details/aberdeenuniversi01univuoft

'Stoats Porridge Bar'. www.theskinny.co.uk/article/39253-stoats-porridge-bar

Irn Bru

Slack, Chris, 'No longer to Be Made from Scottish Girders', *Daily Mail*, 28 September 2011. www.dailymail.co.uk/news/article-2042916/Irn-Bru-England-boom-sales.html

Brooks, Libby, 'Scotland's Other National Drink', *Guardian*, 30 May 2007. www.theguardian.com/commentisfree/2007/may/30/scotlandsothernationaldrink

'End of an Era for Iconic Irn-Bru Maker', Sky News, 27 May 2009: 'During the years Irn-Bru has been advertised as '"Scotland's other National Drink", referring to whisky.' news.sky.com/story/695445/end-of-an-era-for-iconic-irn-bru-maker

Archibald, Ben, 'Fanny Business: Thousands of Cheeky Irn Bru Bottles on Sale', *The Sun*, 19 June 2013. www.thescottishsun.co.uk/scotsol/homepage/4974711/Fanny-business-Thousands-of-cheeky-Irn-Bru-bottles-on-sale.html

Ofcom response to complaints about Leith Agency advert for Irn-Bru, July 2004.

'Irn-Bru Foetus Campaign Leaves TV Viewers Fizzing', *The Scotsman*, 15 June 2003.

'Irn-Bru Adverts Shows Scots Father's Nightmare', *The Scotsman*, 13 March 2013 (on the 'Irn-Bru Gets You Through' campaign).

Marles, Gillian, 'Irn Bru Secrets to Be Passed On', BBC News Scotland, 25 May 2009. news.bbc.co.uk/1/hi/scotland/8066968.stm

Boggan, Steve. 'Irn Bru Is New Opiate of the Russian Masses', *Independent*, 29 September 1999. www.independent.co.uk/news/column-one-irn-bru-is-new-opiate-of-the-russian-masses-1122915.html

Piddling Matters

'Ten Stupidest Laws Are Named', *Telegraph*, 12 April 2008.

Tartan Flags in Prominent Places

www.scottishtartans.org/space_tartans.htm

Grace Banks:

Heroes of Old

MacInnes, Revd D., *Waifs and Strays of Celtic Tradition. Volume II: Folk and Hero Tales* (1890).

www.archive.org/stream/worksofossianson01macpiala

www.educationscotland.gov.uk

www.clandonald.com

Lamont-Brown, Raymond, *Scottish Folklore* (Birlinn, 1996).

The Big Grey Man of Ben Macdhui

www.biggreyman.co.uk
www.scottishhills.com

The Coffin Wrangle

Stewart, Sheila, *Pilgrims of the Mist* (Birlinn, 2008).

From around the Fortingall Yew

Wheater, Hilary, *Aberfeldy to Glen Lyon* (Appin, 1981).

There and Back Again

Hamilton, Ian, *Stone of Destiny* (Birlinn, 2008).

Dark Tower, Dark Tales

Low, Leonard, *The Weem Witch* (Steve Savage, 2006).

Influence from the Other Side

reformationhistory.org/patrickhamilton.html
www.ccel.org/f/foxe/martyrs/fox115.htm

Rogue and Reiver

Murray, W.H., *Rob Roy Macgregor* (Canongate, 2000).

One Good Turn

Blair, Anna, *Scottish Tales* (Chambers, 1991).

The Fairies Craftsman

Warner, Gerald, *Tales of the Scottish Highlands* (Shepheard-Walwyn, 1982).

A Hollow Victory

www.historic-scotland.gov.uk

A Boon or Herald of Doom?

Wilson, Barbara Ker, *Scottish Folk Tales and Legends* (Oxford University Press, 1989).
www.pitt.edu/~dash/dunvegan.html
Lockhart, J.G., *Memoirs of the Life of Sir Walter Scott* (Adam and Charles Black, 1852), p.282.
faeryfolklorist.blogspot.co.uk/2013/02/the-fairy-flag-of-dunvegan-castle-skye.html
www.dunvegancastle.com/content/default.asp?page=s2_5

Finders but Not Keepers

www.kildonanmuseum.co.uk
Humphreys, Rob and Donald Reid, *The Rough Guide to Scottish Highlands & Islands* (Rough Guides, 2011).

Miers, Richenda, *Scotland's Highlands and Islands* (Cadogan Guides, 2006).
www.britainexpress.com/scotland/Highlands/ancient/index.htm?page=5

Ardvreck Castle

Miller, Hugh, *Scenes and Legends of the North of Scotland* (Adam and Charles Black, 1835).
Westwood, Jennifer and Sophie Kingshill, *The Lore of Scotland: A Guide to Scottish Legends* (Random House, 2009).
www.britainexpress.com/scotland/Highlands/Sutherland/Ardvreck-Castle.htm
Pegg, Bob, *Highland Folk Tales* (History Press, 2012).

The Great Serpent of the North

Jarvie, Gordon (ed.), *Scottish Folk and Fairy Tales* (Penguin, 1997).

The Loch Ness Monster and Other Tales

Adamnan of Iona (trans. Richard Sharpe), *Life of Columba* (Penguin Classics, 1995), p.176.
Grant Stewart, W., *The Popular Superstitions and Festive Amusements of the Highlanders of Scotland* (1823).
Watson, Roland, *The Water Horses of Loch Ness* (Createspace, 2011).
lochnessmystery.blogspot.co.uk/2013/04/a-report-on-80th-year-of-nessie.html
www.mirror.co.uk/news/uk-news/loch-ness-monster-sighting-freakish-2224269
www.bbc.co.uk/news/uk-scotland-highlands-islands-21574832#story_continues_2
www.dailyrecord.co.uk/news/weird-news/tourists-shock-morag-loch-morar-2219656
www.cfz.org.uk/expeditions/morag/morag.htm
Campbell, Elizabeth and David Solomon, *The Search for Morag* (1972).
lochnessmystery.blogspot.co.uk/2012/03/some-tales-of-mhorag-of-loch-morar.html

In the Wrong Camp

www.aboutaberdeen.com/culloden-ghosts.php
www.information-britain.co.uk/loredetail.php

A Vicious Torture

Forrest, Liz, *The History of the Churches of Kinlochewe, Wester Ross* (August 2002).

The Black Sail of Loch Maree

Dixon, J.H., *Gairloch and Guide to Loch Maree* (1886; reprinted Gairloch and District Heritage Society, 2004).
www.electricscotland.com/history/gairloch/g204.htm

The Second Sight

Sutherland, Alex, *The Brahan Seer: The Making of a Legend* (Peer Lang, 2009).

Miller, Hugh, *Scenes and Legends of the North of Scotland* (Adam and Charles Black, 1835).

Mackenzie, Alexander, *The Prophecies of the Brahan Seer* (A. & W. Mackenzie, 1878).